Northern California Travel Guide

BnW Travel Series

Ashok Kumawat

Disclaimer: The information provided in this Northern California travel guide is based on research, personal experiences, and the knowledge available. While every effort has been made to ensure the accuracy of the information presented, travel conditions, attractions, and services may change over time. Readers are advised to independently verify the current status, opening hours, and accessibility of attractions, accommodations, and other points of interest mentioned in this guide. The author and publisher are not responsible for any inaccuracies, omissions, or losses incurred as a result of using this guide. Travelers are encouraged to exercise caution, follow local laws and regulations, and prioritize personal safety during their visit to Northern California.

Table of contents:

Introduction to Northern California

Welcome to the breathtaking region of Northern California, a land of remarkable diversity and natural beauty. Nestled between the Pacific Ocean and the towering Sierra Nevada Mountains, this enchanting destination offers a multitude of experiences for every type of traveler. From vibrant cities to serene coastal towns, lush forests to arid deserts, and world-class vineyards to iconic national parks, Northern California truly has something for everyone.

Geographically, Northern California encompasses a vast area, stretching from the Oregon border in the north to the Central Valley in the south. It is comprised of diverse regions, each with its own unique charm and attractions. In this travel guide, we will embark on a journey through this captivating land, discovering its hidden gems, iconic landmarks, and unforgettable experiences.

Our adventure begins in San Francisco, the cultural hub and heart of Northern California. Known for its iconic Golden Gate Bridge, eclectic neighborhoods, and vibrant food scene, San Francisco is a city that effortlessly blends history and innovation. Take a stroll along the bustling waterfront at Fisherman's Wharf, savor a delicious clam chowder in a sourdough bread bowl, and ride a historic cable car up the city's hilly streets for breathtaking views. Delve into the city's rich history at Alcatraz Island, once home to infamous criminals, and explore the bohemian spirit of the

Haight-Ashbury neighborhood, the birthplace of the counterculture movement.

As we venture beyond the city, we find ourselves in the picturesque Napa Valley, a haven for wine enthusiasts. With its rolling vineyards, elegant wineries, and world-renowned wine tasting experiences, Napa Valley offers a sensory journey like no other. Immerse yourself in the art of winemaking, sample exquisite vintages, and indulge in gourmet cuisine paired with the perfect wine. The region's beauty extends beyond the vineyards, with hot air balloon rides providing breathtaking aerial views and the charming town of Yountville offering delightful shopping and dining experiences.

Continuing our exploration, we follow the rugged coastline to discover the natural wonders of Northern California. The Pacific Coast Highway beckons with its scenic beauty, winding along dramatic cliffs and pristine beaches. Discover the rugged beauty of Big Sur, where majestic cliffs meet the crashing waves of the Pacific Ocean. Explore the charming coastal towns of Mendocino and Half Moon Bay, where idyllic beaches, art galleries, and quaint shops await. Breathe in the fresh ocean air and be captivated by the coastal magic that defines this region.

No visit to Northern California would be complete without venturing into the enchanting realm of the redwoods. Humboldt Redwoods State Park and Muir Woods National Monument are home to towering ancient trees that inspire awe and reverence. Walking among these giants is a humbling experience, connecting us with nature in its most majestic form. Feel the serenity as sunlight filters through the dense canopy, illuminating a world of vibrant greens and tranquil silence.

Nature lovers will find their paradise in the Sierra Nevada Mountains, home to the crown jewel of California's national parks – Yosemite. With its breathtaking waterfalls, towering granite cliffs, and diverse ecosystems, Yosemite National Park offers endless opportunities for exploration. Hike through lush meadows, witness the power of Yosemite Falls, and marvel at the iconic Half Dome. Experience the park's grandeur and connect with the raw beauty of the natural world.

Beyond the wilderness, Northern California boasts vibrant cities and unique destinations. Sacramento, the state capital, blends a rich history with modern urban amenities. Explore the historic Old Sacramento district, visit the captivating California State Capitol, and enjoy the city's flourishing farm-to-fork culinary scene. Further south, the tech hub of Silicon Valley beckons with its innovative spirit. Discover the world-changing technologies that have shapedour modern lives, visit iconic companies like Apple and Google, and immerse yourself in the cutting-edge culture of innovation.

Northern California also holds a rich historical

legacy, particularly in the Gold Country region. Travel back in time to the era of the California Gold Rush and explore charming towns like Auburn, Nevada City, and Placerville. Pan for gold in the American River, visit well-preserved historic sites, and immerse yourself in the stories of the pioneers who sought their fortunes in the gold mines.

For outdoor enthusiasts, Northern California offers a playground of adventure. Whether it's hiking the stunning trails of Lake Tahoe, skiing down powdery slopes in the winter, or kayaking on picturesque rivers, there is no shortage of activities to get your adrenaline pumping. The Shasta Cascade region boasts numerous lakes, waterfalls, and volcanic landscapes, providing endless opportunities for exploration and outdoor recreation.

Food and wine lovers will find their bliss in Northern California's culinary scene. From farm-to-table restaurants serving fresh and locally sourced ingredients to vibrant farmers' markets showcasing the region's abundance, Northern California delights the taste buds. Indulge in the flavors of Sonoma County, known for its award-winning wines and farm-fresh produce, or savor the delectable seafood of the Monterey Bay area.

Throughout this guide, we will delve into the various regions of Northern California, offering insider tips, detailed itineraries, and recommendations to help you make the most of your visit. Whether you're seeking natural wonders, cultural immersion, culinary delights, or outdoor adventures, Northern California promises a memorable journey filled with awe-inspiring landscapes, vibrant cities, and warm hospitality.

As you embark on this exploration of Northern California, prepare to be enchanted by its diverse landscapes, captivated by its rich history, and inspired by its spirit of innovation. Get ready to create unforgettable memories in this remarkable region that truly has it all. Let the adventure begin!

Planning Your Northern California Adventure

Embarking on a journey to Northern California promises an unforgettable adventure filled with breathtaking landscapes, vibrant cities, and a multitude of activities to suit every traveler's taste. To ensure a seamless and enjoyable trip, careful planning is essential. In this chapter, we will guide you through the key aspects of planning your Northern California adventure, from choosing the right time to visit to arranging transportation and accommodations.

Deciding the Best Time to Visit:

Northern California experiences a mild climate, with regional variations. The summer months from June to August offer warm and sunny weather, making it an ideal time for outdoor activities and exploring the coastal regions. Spring (March to May) and fall (September to November) bring pleasant temperatures, fewer crowds, and the opportunity to witness stunning wildflower blooms and fall foliage. Winter (December to February) brings cooler temperatures, particularly in the mountainous regions, and is perfect for winter sports enthusiasts or those seeking a peaceful getaway.

Duration of Your Stay:

Consider the length of your stay when planning your itinerary. Northern California offers a wealth of attractions, from vibrant cities to natural wonders, so allow ample time to explore each region thoroughly. A minimum of one week is recommended to cover the major highlights, but extending your trip to two weeks or more will allow for a more in-depth exploration and the opportunity to discover hidden gems off the beaten path.

Creating Your Itinerary:

Research and prioritize the destinations and activities that interest you the most. San Francisco, Napa Valley, Yosemite National Park, and the coastal highway are among the must-visit attractions. Consider your preferences—whether you enjoy outdoor adventures, cultural experiences, or a mix of both—and design an itinerary that aligns with your interests. Be realistic about the time needed to fully appreciate each destination, allowing for leisurely exploration and unexpected discoveries along the way.

Transportation:

Northern California is well-connected by air, with major airports in San Francisco, Sacramento, and San Jose. Depending on your arrival point and itinerary, renting a car may be the most convenient option for exploring the region, particularly if you plan to venture into national parks and remote areas. Public transportation, including buses and trains, can be an alternative for urban exploration and short-distance travel.

Accommodations:

Consider the diverse range of accommodations available throughout Northern California. From luxurious hotels and resorts to charming bed and breakfasts, vacation rentals, and campgrounds, there are options to suit every budget and travel style. In popular destinations like San Francisco and Napa Valley, booking accommodations in advance is advisable, especially during peak travel seasons. Research the different areas within each destination to find the location that best suits your preferences and allows easy access to your planned activities.

Packing Essentials:

Northern California's varied climate necessitates packing a range of clothing options. Layered clothing is key, as temperatures can fluctuate throughout the day. In coastal regions, a light jacket or sweater is recommended, even during the summer. Comfortable walking shoes are a must for exploring cities and natural attractions. If you plan to visit national parks or engage in outdoor activities, pack appropriate gear such as hiking boots, sunscreen, hats, and water bottles. Don't forget your camera to capture the stunning landscapes and memorable moments.

Researching Activities and Attractions:

To make the most of your time in Northern California, research the activities and attractions that align with your interests. From wine tasting in Napa Valley to hiking in Yosemite National Park, there is an abundance of experiences to choose from. Look into guided tours, outdoor adventures, cultural events, and local festivals happening during your visit. Planning ahead allows you to secure reservations for popular activities and make the most efficient use of your time.

Budgeting and Expenses:

Consider your budget and allocate funds forvarious expenses such as transportation, accommodations, meals, activities, and souvenirs. Northern California offers a wide range of options to suit different budgets, so plan accordingly. Research admission fees, parking costs, and any additional expenses associated with your chosen activities to avoid surprises. It's also a good idea to set aside some extra funds for unexpected expenses or spontaneous adventures that may arise during your trip.

Safety and Health:

Prioritize your safety and well-being during your Northern California adventure. Familiarize yourself with local laws and regulations, and take necessary precautions when exploring natural areas or engaging in outdoor activities. Check the weather conditions and follow any safety advisories or warnings. It's always a good idea to have travel insurance that covers medical emergencies and trip cancellations.

Embracing Flexibility:

While careful planning is essential, it's also important to embrace flexibility and allow for spontaneity during your Northern California adventure. Leave room in your itinerary for unexpected detours, local recommendations, and serendipitous discoveries. Sometimes the most memorable experiences come from stepping off the beaten path and embracing the unknown.

By taking these key aspects into consideration and planning your Northern California adventure with care, you'll set the stage for an incredible and seamless journey. From the bustling streets of San Francisco to the tranquil beauty of Yosemite National Park, Northern California awaits, ready to captivate you with its natural wonders, cultural treasures, and unforgettable experiences. Get ready to embark on the adventure of a lifetime in this diverse and enchanting region.

Essential Travel Tips for Northern California

Traveling to Northern California offers a world of incredible experiences and natural wonders. To make the most of your journey, it's essential to be well-prepared and equipped with valuable travel tips. In this chapter, we will provide you with essential advice and insights to ensure a smooth and enjoyable adventure in Northern California.

Dress in Layers:

Northern California's climate can vary significantly throughout the day and between different regions. Dressing in layers allows you to adjust to changing temperatures. Carry a light jacket or sweater, even during the summer, as coastal areas can be cool and breezy. In mountainous regions, particularly around Yosemite, be prepared for cooler temperatures and pack warmer clothing.

Be Mindful of Traffic:

Cities like San Francisco and Sacramento can experience heavy traffic, especially during rush hours. Plan your activities accordingly and allow extra time for potential delays. Consider using public transportation or rideshare services to avoid parking hassles and traffic congestion in urban areas.

Consider Off-Peak Travel:

To avoid crowds and higher prices, consider visiting popular destinations like San Francisco, Napa Valley, and Yosemite National Park during the off-peak seasons. Spring and fall generally offer milder weather and fewer tourists, allowing you to explore attractions with more ease and enjoy discounted rates on accommodations.

Make Reservations in Advance:

For popular attractions, such as Alcatraz Island, wine tours in Napa Valley, or guided hikes in Yosemite, it is advisable to make reservations well in advance. These activities often have limited availability, particularly during peak travel seasons. Research and secure your bookings to ensure you don't miss out on the experiences you desire.

Embrace Outdoor Exploration:

Northern California is renowned for its stunning natural landscapes and outdoor activities. Take advantage of the region's offerings by exploring hiking trails, biking routes, and scenic drives. Pack comfortable walking shoes, sunscreen, hats, and reusable water bottles to stay hydrated while venturing into nature.

Respect Nature and Wildlife:

When exploring Northern California's natural areas, it's crucial to respect the environment and wildlife. Follow park rules and regulations, stay on designated trails, and dispose of waste responsibly. Do not feed or approach wild animals, as it can be harmful to both you and the animals. Appreciate the beauty of nature while preserving it for future generations.

Stay Hydrated:

Northern California's climate can be dry, particularly in areas like the Central Valley and the Sierra Nevada region. It's important to stay hydrated, especially when engaging in outdoor activities. Carry a reusable water bottle and drink plenty of water throughout the day to prevent dehydration.

Check for Fire and Weather Updates:

Northern California is prone to wildfires, particularly during the dry summer months. Stay informed about fire conditions and check for any travel advisories or warnings before heading to national parks or forested areas. Additionally, keep an eye on weather forecasts, particularly if you plan to visit coastal areas, as fog and coastal breezes can impact visibility and temperatures.

Enjoy the Local Cuisine:

Northern California is a food lover's paradise, renowned for its farm-to-table cuisine, seafood, and world-class wines. Embrace the local culinary scene by sampling fresh produce at farmers' markets, indulging in seafood delights along the coast, and exploring the diverse dining options in cities like San Francisco and Sacramento. Don't forget to try the region's famous wines in Napa Valley, Sonoma County, and Mendocino.

Stay Connected:

Having a reliable internet connection can be beneficial while traveling in Northern California. Keep your mobile devices charged and consider purchasing a local SIM card or activating an international roaming plan to stay connected. Utilize travel apps and online maps to navigate the region, find nearby attractions, and stay updated on transportation schedules.

Practice Responsible Wine Tasting:

If you plan to explore the wineries of Napa Valley or other wine regions in Northern California, practice responsible wine tasting. Designate a driver or consider booking a wine tour that includes transportation. It's important to enjoy the experience safely and avoid drinking and driving.

Be Prepared for Coastal Conditions:

Northern California's coastline can be subject to fog, strong winds, and chilly temperatures, even during the summer. Pack appropriate clothing, including windbreakers or jackets, when visiting coastal areas. Embrace the beauty of the dramatic coastal landscapes while being prepared for the weather conditions.

Respect Local Customs and Etiquette:

When visiting Northern California, respect the local customs and etiquette. Californians are generally known for their relaxed and friendly demeanor. Practice common courtesy, observe any local customs, and be mindful of the environment and local communities.

Stay Sun-Safe:

Even on overcast days, the sun's rays can be strong in Northern California. Protect yourself from sunburn by wearing sunscreen, sunglasses, and a hat. Seek shade during the hottest parts of the day and stay hydrated to avoid heat-related issues.

Stay Safe in Urban Areas:

While Northern California's cities are generally safe for travelers, it's always wise to take precautions. Be aware of your surroundings, particularly in crowded areas or tourist spots. Keep your belongings secure and avoid displaying valuable items. If you're unfamiliar with a neighborhood, consult local resources or ask for recommendations to ensure a safe and enjoyable urban experience.

Pack a Daypack for Exploration:

Carry a lightweight daypack for your daily adventures. Pack essentials such as water, snacks, sunscreen, a map, a small first aid kit, and a portable charger for your electronic devices. A daypack allows you to carry your belongings comfortably and have everything you need for a day of exploration.

Engage with Local Communities:

Northern California is home to diverse communities, each with its own culture and heritage. Embrace the opportunity to engage with locals, learn about their traditions, and support local businesses. Attend local events or festivals to immerse yourself in the vibrant spirit of the region.

Be Mindful of Water Conservation:

Northern California occasionally experiences drought conditions. Be mindful of water usage, particularly in areas where water scarcity may be a concern. Conserve water by taking shorter showers, reusing towels, and minimizing water waste whenever possible.

Stay Informed about COVID-19 Guidelines:

During your trip to Northern California, stay informed about the latest COVID-19 guidelines and restrictions. Check government websites, local health advisories, and the official websites of attractions or accommodations for updated information. Follow recommended safety protocols, including wearing masks, practicing social distancing, and adhering to capacity limits when visiting indoor establishments.

Have a Sense of Adventure and Openness:

Finally, approach your Northern California adventure with a sense of adventure and openness. Embrace the diversity of experiences, try new activities, and be open to unexpected discoveries. Northern California is a region of wonder and surprises, and by embracing its spirit, you're sure to create cherished memories.

By following these essential travel tips, you'll be well-prepared to embark on an incredible journey through Northern California. From its stunning landscapes to its vibrant cities, this region is ready to captivate you with its beauty, charm, and rich cultural heritage. Pack your bags, plan your itinerary, and get ready for an unforgettable adventure in Northern California.

Exploring San Francisco: The City by the Bay

Welcome to San Francisco, the vibrant and culturally rich city that has captured the hearts of visitors from around the world. Nestled on the hilly terrain of Northern California, this iconic destination offers a unique blend of natural beauty, architectural wonders, and a thriving cultural scene. In this chapter, we will take you on a journey through San Francisco, highlighting its must-visit attractions, neighborhoods, culinary delights, and the essence that makes it truly one-of-a-kind.

The Golden Gate Bridge:

No visit to San Francisco is complete without marveling at the majestic Golden Gate Bridge. This iconic symbol of the city spans the entrance to the San Francisco Bay, offering breathtaking views and photo opportunities. Take a stroll or rent a bike to cross the bridge, or explore the nearby Presidio, a former military base turned park with scenic trails and historic sites.

Fisherman's Wharf and Pier 39:

Immerse yourself in the bustling atmosphere of Fisherman's Wharf, a vibrant waterfront district teeming with shops, restaurants, and attractions. Indulge in fresh seafood delicacies, such as clam chowder served in a sourdough bread bowl or Dungeness crab. Don't miss the playful sea lions that have made Pier 39 their home, delighting visitors with their antics.

Alcatraz Island:

Step into history with a visit to Alcatraz Island, once home to one of the most notorious federal penitentiaries. Take a ferry from Fisherman's Wharf to explore the island and its former prison, where infamous criminals like Al Capone were incarcerated. The audio-guided tour provides fascinating insights into the prison's history, offering a glimpse into the lives of inmates and the challenges they faced.

Exploring Neighborhoods:

San Francisco is a city of diverse and vibrant neighborhoods, each with its own character and charm. Visit the colorful Victorian houses of Alamo Square, known as the "Painted Ladies," and capture a picture-perfect view of the city skyline. Explore the bohemian ambiance of the Haight-Ashbury district, the epicenter of the counterculture movement in the 1960s. Wander through the vibrant streets of Chinatown, the largest Chinese community outside of Asia, and indulge in authentic cuisine and unique shopping experiences.

The Embarcadero:

Stroll along the Embarcadero, San Francisco's scenic waterfront promenade. Enjoy panoramic views of the bay, encounter street performers, and explore the Ferry Building Marketplace, a food lover's paradise with artisanal shops and a bustling farmers' market. Don't forget to try the famous clam chowder in a bread bowl at one of the waterfront seafood stands.

Cable Cars and Lombard Street:

Experience the charm of San Francisco's historic cable cars, a true symbol of the city's transportation heritage. Hop on a cable car and enjoy a thrilling ride up the steep hills, passing by iconic sights along the way. Make a stop at Lombard Street, often called the "crookedest street in the world," known for its picturesque curves and vibrant flowerbeds.

Museums and Cultural Institutions:

San Francisco boasts an array of world-class museums and cultural institutions. Visit the de Young Museum in Golden Gate Park, showcasing American art and international exhibitions. Explore the Asian Art Museum, home to an extensive collection of Asian art and artifacts. Immerse yourself in contemporary art at the San Francisco Museum of Modern Art (SFMOMA). These are just a few examples of the city's rich cultural landscape.

Golden Gate Park:

Escape the hustle and bustle of the city and find tranquility in Golden Gate Park. This sprawling urban oasis offers a wealth of attractionsand activities. Explore the Japanese Tea Garden, a serene and picturesque retreat. Visit the California Academy of Sciences, an interactive science museum with a planetarium and an aquarium. Take a leisurely stroll through the park's beautiful gardens, enjoy a picnic, or rent a paddleboat on Stow Lake.

Culinary Delights:

San Francisco is a paradise for food lovers, with a culinary scene that reflects its diverse population and cultural influences. Indulge in the city's famous sourdough bread, taste the fresh seafood at renowned restaurants on the waterfront, or embark on a culinary adventure in neighborhoods like the Mission District, known for its vibrant food scene. Don't forget to try the city's beloved chocolate treats and artisanal ice cream.

Performing Arts and Nightlife:

San Francisco's vibrant performing arts scene offers a wealth of entertainment options. Catch a show at the historic Orpheum Theatre or the iconic Castro Theatre, known for its classic movie screenings. Enjoy live music performances at renowned venues like The Fillmore or the Great American Music Hall. In the evening, explore the city's lively nightlife scene, from trendy cocktail bars in the Mission District to jazz clubs in North Beach.

Outdoor Activities:

San Francisco's mild climate and natural surroundings provide ample opportunities for outdoor activities. Take a scenic bike ride along the waterfront or through Golden Gate Park. Go for a hike in the nearby Marin Headlands or enjoy a day at one of the city's picturesque beaches, such as Ocean Beach or Baker Beach.

Festivals and Events:

Throughout the year, San Francisco hosts an

array of festivals and events that celebrate its diverse culture and heritage. From the lively Chinese New Year Parade to the colorful Pride Parade and the vibrant Carnaval, there's always something happening in the city. Check the local event calendar and plan your visit to coincide with these unique celebrations.

As you explore San Francisco, immerse yourself in the city's vibrant spirit, embrace its cultural diversity, and be open to new experiences. Whether you're traversing the iconic Golden Gate Bridge, savoring local cuisine, or wandering through its eclectic neighborhoods, San Francisco will captivate you with its charm and leave a lasting impression. Enjoy the sights, sounds, and flavors of this remarkable city by the bay.

Napa Valley: A Wine Lover's Paradise

Welcome to Napa Valley, a captivating region nestled in the heart of Northern California, renowned worldwide as a haven for wine enthusiasts. With its rolling vineyards, picturesque landscapes, and award-winning wineries, Napa Valley offers a wine lover's paradise like no other. In this chapter, we will guide you through the essence of Napa Valley, highlighting its winemaking heritage, notable wineries, breathtaking scenery, and the unforgettable experiences that make it a must-visit destination for wine connoisseurs and enthusiasts alike.

A Rich Winemaking Legacy:

Napa Valley has a long and storied winemaking history that dates back to the 19th century. This region's commitment to quality and innovation has helped establish its reputation as one of the world's premier wine regions. Explore the history and heritage of Napa Valley's winemaking through guided tours, visits to historic estates, and engaging with winemakers who passionately share their knowledge and craft.

Vineyard Landscapes and Terroir:

The landscapes of Napa Valley are a sight to behold. Rolling hills, verdant vineyards, and idyllic countryside vistas create a picturesque backdrop for wine tasting and exploration. Take a leisurely drive along the scenic Silverado Trail or the famous Highway 29, which winds its way through the valley, offering stunning views of vineyard-covered hills and charming wineries. Immerse yourself in the beauty of the region and appreciate the unique terroir that contributes to the exceptional quality of Napa Valley wines.

Wine Tasting Experiences:

Napa Valley offers an array of wine tasting experiences, ranging from intimate boutique wineries to grand estates. From the moment you step into a tasting room, you'll be greeted by knowledgeable staff eager to share their passion for winemaking. Explore a variety of wine varietals, from the classic Cabernet Sauvignon and Chardonnay to lesser-known gems like Merlot, Zinfandel, and Sauvignon Blanc. Discover the nuances of each wine as you learn about the winemaking process, vineyard practices, and the art of wine blending.

Wine Train and Vineyard Excursions:

Embark on a unique wine tasting journey aboard the Napa Valley Wine Train, a restored vintage train that takes you on a scenic ride through the valley. Enjoy gourmet cuisine paired with fine wines as you pass by vineyards and wineries. Alternatively, opt for a vineyard excursion, where you can visit wineries by bike, hot air balloon, or even horse-drawn carriage, allowing you to immerse yourself in the beauty of the vineyards up close.

Culinary Delights and Wine Pairings:

Napa Valley's culinary scene is as exquisite as its wines. Indulge in farm-to-table dining experiences, where local ingredients are paired with the region's finest wines. Many wineries offer food and wine pairing experiences, where expertly crafted dishes complement the flavors of their wines. From Michelin-starred restaurants to casual bistros, Napa Valley's dining options will delight your palate and enhance your wine tasting adventures.

Wine Education and Classes:

Expand your wine knowledge with educational experiences and classes offered in Napa Valley. Join winemaking workshops, blending sessions, or vineyard tours led by experts who will guide you through the intricacies of winemaking and grape growing. Learn about the different appellations within Napa Valley, the impact of soil and climate on wine characteristics, and the art of wine appreciation.

Harvest Season and Wine Festivals:

Experience the magic of the grape harvest season in Napa Valley, typically taking place from August to October. Witness the vineyards come alive with activity as grapes arecarefully handpicked and transformed into wine. Participate in grape stomping events, harvest celebrations, and winery tours that offer behind-the-scenes glimpses into the winemaking process during this exciting time. Additionally, Napa Valley hosts various wine festivals and events throughout the year, where you can taste a wide selection of wines, attend seminars, and engage with winemakers and industry experts.

Sustainable and Organic Practices:

Napa Valley is at the forefront of sustainable and organic winemaking practices. Many wineries embrace environmentally friendly approaches, including organic farming, biodynamic viticulture, and solar energy utilization. Visit certified sustainable wineries to learn about their commitment to eco-friendly practices and the importance of preserving the land for future generations.

Art and Culture:

Napa Valley's wine country is not only known for its vineyards but also for its vibrant art and cultural scene. Explore the region's art galleries, sculpture gardens, and performance venues. Visit the Hess Collection, a winery that houses a remarkable contemporary art collection, or enjoy a live performance at the Napa Valley Opera House. The intersection of art and wine creates a unique and enriching experience for visitors.

Luxury Accommodations and Spas:

Extend your stay in Napa Valley by indulging in luxury accommodations and world-class spas. From boutique hotels and charming bed and breakfasts to renowned resorts, there are options to suit every taste. Unwind with vineyard views, rejuvenate with vinotherapy spa treatments, and savor the tranquility of the valley's serene surroundings.

Napa Valley's allure as a wine lover's paradise

is undeniable. Its dedication to winemaking excellence, breathtaking landscapes, and unforgettable experiences make it a destination that leaves a lasting impression. Whether you're an experienced oenophile or a curious wine enthusiast, Napa Valley invites you to savor its rich flavors, embrace its beauty, and create memories that will be cherished long after your visit. Cheers to an extraordinary wine journey in Napa Valley!

Coastal Delights: Discovering the Northern California Coastline

Welcome to the stunning Northern California coastline, where rugged cliffs, pristine beaches, and breathtaking vistas await you. This chapter will guide you through the coastal delights of this mesmerizing region, from iconic landmarks to hidden gems that will leave you in awe. Prepare to embark on a journey of exploration, immersing yourself in the natural beauty, charming coastal towns, and unforgettable experiences that make the Northern California coastline a true paradise for nature lovers and adventure seekers.

The Pacific Coast Highway:

The Pacific Coast Highway, also known as Highway 1, is a scenic roadway that winds along the coast, offering panoramic views at every turn. Drive along this iconic route, passing through quaint towns, dramatic cliffs, and picturesque coves. Be prepared for stunning vistas of the Pacific Ocean, with opportunities to stop at lookout points and capture breathtaking photographs.

Big Sur:

One of the most enchanting stretches of the Northern California coastline is Big Sur. This rugged region is characterized by towering cliffs, pristine beaches, and majestic coastal forests. Take a leisurely drive through this awe-inspiring landscape, stopping at notable landmarks like Bixby Creek Bridge and McWay Falls. Explore hiking trails that lead to hidden coves and panoramic viewpoints, allowing you to fully immerse yourself in Big Sur's natural wonders.

Mendocino and the Lost Coast:

Discover the idyllic beauty of Mendocino, a charming coastal town known for its stunning Victorian architecture and artistic community. Stroll along the rugged cliffs, explore the boutiques and art galleries, and indulge in gourmet cuisine. Further north, explore the secluded wilderness of the Lost Coast, a remote and untouched stretch of coastline that offers unmatched tranquility and beauty.

Point Reyes National Seashore:

Point Reyes National Seashore is a coastal gem, showcasing diverse ecosystems and captivating landscapes. Explore its sandy beaches, hike through lush forests, and witness the dramatic collision of land and sea at Point Reyes Lighthouse. Keep an eye out for wildlife, as the area is home to numerous species, including elephant seals, tule elk, and a variety of bird species.

Coastal Towns and Beaches:

Northern California's coastal towns offer a charming escape from the bustling city life. Visit the laid-back town of Half Moon Bay, known for its pumpkin festivals and picturesque coastline. Experience the bohemian vibe of Bolinas, a hidden gem where time seems to stand still. Explore the quaint town of Mendocino, with its romantic bed and breakfasts and stunning coastal views. Relax on the sandy beaches of Santa Cruz, known for its surf culture and beachside amusement park.

Whale Watching and Marine Life:

The Northern California coastline is a haven for marine life, offering opportunities for unforgettable encounters. Join a whale-watching excursion, particularly during the migration season (spring and fall), to witness majestic gray whales, humpbacks, or even orcas as they journey along the coast. Keep an eye out for sea otters, harbor seals, and dolphins that call these waters home.

State and National Parks:

Northern California's coastline is dotted with remarkable state and national parks that preserve its natural treasures. Visit Julia Pfeiffer Burns State Park to witness McWay Falls cascading onto a pristine beach, or explore Salt Point State Park, known for its rugged cliffs and tide pools. Further north, explore Redwood National and State Parks, where ancient giants tower over the coastline, creating a truly magical experience.

Outdoor Activities:

The Northern California coastline offers a wealth of outdoor activities for adventure enthusiasts. Embark on coastal hikes, paddle along tranquil estuaries, or try your hand at surfing on renowned breaks. Kayaking, beachcombing, horseback riding, and camping arealso popular activities that allow you to fully immerse yourself in the coastal environment.

Fresh Seafood and Local Cuisine:

Indulge in the bounty of the sea along the Northern California coastline. Sample fresh oysters in Tomales Bay, savor Dungeness crab in Mendocino, or enjoy a seafood feast in a charming coastal town. Explore local farmers' markets to discover fresh produce, artisanal cheeses, and other delectable treats. Don't forget to pair your meals with local wines, as many coastal areas have thriving vineyards and wineries nearby.

Sunset Spectacles:

Witnessing the sunset along the Northern California coastline is a truly magical experience. Find a secluded spot on a beach, perch atop a cliff, or simply enjoy the view from a waterfront restaurant. As the sun dips below the horizon, the sky paints a canvas of vibrant colors, creating a captivating and serene moment that will leave a lasting impression.

Sustainable Tourism and Conservation:

As you explore the Northern California coastline, it's important to practice sustainable tourism and contribute to the preservation of this remarkable environment. Respect nature and wildlife, dispose of waste responsibly, and follow any regulations or guidelines in place to protect fragile ecosystems. Support local businesses and initiatives that prioritize sustainability, ensuring that future generations can continue to enjoy the beauty of the coastline.

Hidden Gems and Serendipitous Discoveries:

One of the joys of exploring the Northern California coastline is stumbling upon hidden gems and serendipitous discoveries. Take the time to wander off the beaten path, explore lesser-known beaches, and engage with the locals to uncover the region's best-kept secrets. Whether it's stumbling upon a secluded cove, encountering a local art exhibit, or discovering a hidden coastal trail, these unexpected moments will add an extra layer of magic to your coastal adventure.

The Northern California coastline beckons with its rugged beauty, diverse ecosystems, and coastal charm. From the iconic landmarks of Big Sur to the tranquility of Point Reyes and the enchanting coastal towns in between, this region invites you to explore, unwind, and connect with the natural wonders that make it truly extraordinary. Embrace the coastal delights of Northern California and create memories that will last a lifetime.

The Majestic Redwoods: Journey into Ancient Forests

Welcome to the awe-inspiring world of the majestic redwoods, where towering giants beckon visitors into a realm of ancient beauty and tranquility. In this chapter, we invite you to embark on a journey into the enchanting forests of Northern California, where the mighty coast redwoods and giant sequoias stand as living testaments to the resilience and grandeur of nature. Prepare to be captivated by their towering heights, serene groves, and the profound sense of wonder that these ancient forests inspire.

The Coast Redwoods: Towering Giants of the Coastline

The coast redwoods (Sequoia sempervirens) are the tallest living organisms on Earth, reaching heights of over 350 feet (107 meters). Experience the awe-inspiring beauty of these majestic trees as you wander through the coastal redwood forests. Visit iconic parks like Muir Woods National Monument, where you can marvel at the sheer size and age of these ancient beings. The serene trails wind through the forest, offering a peaceful escape and an opportunity to connect with the natural world.

The Giant Sequoias: Giants of the Sierra Nevada

Venture into the Sierra Nevada Mountains to discover the giant sequoias (Sequoiadendron giganteum), the most massive trees on the planet.

Explore the world-renowned Sequoia and Kings Canyon National Parks, home to groves of these awe-inspiring giants. Stand beneath the towering sequoias, such as General Sherman, the largest tree by volume in the world, and feel the humbling power of nature's creations.

The Old-Growth Forests: A Window into the Past

Immerse yourself in the magic of the old-growth forests, where time seems to stand still. These ancient forests are characterized by untouched ecosystems that have remained virtually unchanged for centuries. Traverse the trails that wind through these pristine groves, and be transported back in time as you witness the magnificent interplay of light and shadow beneath the towering canopy. These forests offer a glimpse into the rich biodiversity and delicate balance of nature.

Hiking and Exploring the Forests:

Embark on scenic hikes that weave through the redwood forests, allowing you to fully immerse yourself in their splendor. Trails such as the Avenue of the Giants in Humboldt Redwoods State Park, the Stout Grove in Jedediah Smith Redwoods State Park, or the Mariposa Grove in Yosemite National Park offer incredible opportunities to witness the towering giants up close. As you wander through the forest, listen to the rustle of leaves, breathe in the crisp forest air, and feel the serenity that envelops these ancient landscapes.

Wildlife and Flora:

The redwood forests are not only home to the towering trees but also a diverse array of wildlife and flora. Look out for black bears, deer, and an abundance of bird species as you explore the forest trails. Marvel at the delicate wildflowers and ferns that carpet the forest floor, adding a splash of color to the verdant surroundings. Keep your eyes and ears open for the melodious songs of birds and the rustle of squirrels, as they go about their lives amidst the grandeur of the forest.

Immersive Nature Centers and Interpretive Programs:

Enhance your understanding of the redwood forests by visiting immersive nature centers and participating in interpretive programs. Parks such as Redwood National and State Parks offer informative visitor centers, where you can learn about the ecology, history, and conservation efforts dedicated to these remarkable ecosystems. Join guided walks, ranger-led programs, or educational workshops to deepen your appreciation for these ancient forests.

Camping and Outdoor Adventures:

Immerse yourself in the tranquility of the redwood forests byembarking on a camping adventure. Numerous campgrounds nestled amidst the redwoods offer a chance to spend a night under the towering canopy, surrounded by the serenity of nature. Wake up to the gentle sounds of the forest, enjoy a campfire beneath the stars, and embark on early morning hikes to witness the forests come alive with the first rays of sunlight.

Canopy Tours and Tree Walks:

For a unique perspective of the redwood forests, consider embarking on a canopy tour or tree walk. These guided experiences allow you to explore the treetops, walking on suspended bridges and platforms that offer breathtaking views of the forest below. Traverse through the branches and gain a newfound appreciation for the intricacies and interconnectedness of the redwood ecosystem.

Conservation and Preservation Efforts:

Learn about the ongoing conservation and preservation efforts dedicated to protecting these ancient forests for future generations. Understand the importance of sustainable practices and responsible tourism to ensure the long-term health and vitality of the redwoods. Support organizations and initiatives that work tirelessly to safeguard these natural wonders.

Reflection and Contemplation:

The redwood forests have a way of instilling a sense of peace and reflection. Take the time to disconnect from the modern world, immerse yourself in the stillness of the forest, and allow the majestic redwoods to inspire contemplation and a deep connection to the natural world. These ancient beings have witnessed centuries of human history, and in their presence, one can't help but feel a profound sense of humility and wonder.

Visiting the redwood forests is an

extraordinary experience that will leave an indelible mark on your soul. These ancient giants, with their resilience and magnificence, remind us of the power and beauty of nature. Take the time to explore, appreciate, and protect these extraordinary landscapes, and allow the redwoods to ignite a lifelong love affair with the natural world. Journey into the ancient forests of Northern California, and immerse yourself in the serenity and grandeur of the majestic redwoods.

Sacramento: California's Capital and Historic Gem

Welcome to Sacramento, the vibrant capital city of California and a historic gem nestled in the heart of Northern California. Known for its rich history, cultural attractions, and thriving culinary scene, Sacramento offers a unique blend of modern amenities and old-world charm. In this chapter, we will guide you through the essence of Sacramento, showcasing its captivating landmarks, diverse neighborhoods, and the remarkable experiences that make it a must-visit destination for travelers.

A Capital City with Historic Roots:

As the capital of California, Sacramento holds a significant place in the state's history. Begin your exploration with a visit to the California State Capitol, where you can take a guided tour to learn about the state's political legacy and admire the stunning architecture of the Capitol building. Explore the Capitol Park surrounding the building, which features beautiful gardens and monuments.

Historic Old Sacramento:

Step back in time as you wander through the streets of Old Sacramento, a National Historic Landmark District. This waterfront neighborhood preserves the city's Gold Rush-era heritage, with its charming wooden sidewalks, horse-drawn carriages, and historic buildings. Explore the Old Sacramento State Historic Park, home to museums, shops, and restaurants that offer a glimpse into the city's past.

Museums and Cultural Institutions:

Sacramento is home to an array of museums and cultural institutions that cater to a variety of interests. Visit the Crocker Art Museum, one of the oldest art museums in the West, to admire its extensive collection of California art and European masterpieces. Explore the California State Railroad Museum, where you can learn about the history of the railroad in California and even take a ride on a historic train. Other notable museums include the California Automobile Museum, the California Museum, and the Sacramento History Museum.

Sutter's Fort State Historic Park:

Delve into the pioneering history of Sacramento with a visit to Sutter's Fort State Historic Park. This reconstructed fort, originally built by John Sutter in the mid-1800s, provides a fascinating glimpse into California's early days. Explore the grounds, learn about the lives of early settlers, and gain insight into the impact of the Gold Rush on the region.

Farm-to-Fork Capital:

Sacramento proudly bears the title of "Farm-to-Fork Capital," celebrating its proximity to the fertile agricultural regions of Northern California. Indulge in farm-fresh cuisine and local specialties at the city's renowned farm-to-fork restaurants. Visit the year-round farmers' markets, such as the Sunday Farmers' Market under the freeway, where you can browse an abundance of fresh produce, artisanal products, and gourmet treats.

The American River Parkway:

Escape the urban hustle and immerse yourself in nature along the American River Parkway. This 23-mile (37-kilometer) stretch of protected land offers a haven for outdoor enthusiasts. Enjoy walking, jogging, or cycling along the scenic trails, or take a leisurely picnic along the riverbank. The parkway is also a popular spot for boating, fishing, and birdwatching.

Vibrant Neighborhoods:

Sacramento boasts a variety of diverse neighborhoods, each with its own unique character and attractions. Explore the Midtown district, known for its lively art scene, trendy shops, and eclectic dining options. Visit the R Street Corridor, a former industrial area transformed into a vibrant hub of breweries, restaurants, and galleries. Venture into the Land Park neighborhood, home to the Sacramento Zoo and the stunning William Land Park. Each neighborhood offers a distinct flavor of Sacramento's local culture and community spirit.

Tower Bridge and Riverfront Promenade:

Marvel at the iconic Tower Bridge, a symbol of Sacramento that spans the Sacramento River, connecting the city to West Sacramento. Take a stroll along the Riverfront Promenade, a scenic pathway that meanders along the river's edge. Enjoy picturesque views of the city skyline, watch boats pass by, and soak in the relaxed ambiance of the waterfront.

State-of-the-Art Entertainment:

Sacramento is home to state-of-the-art entertainment venues that host a wide range of events throughout the year. Catch a concert or sporting event at the Golden 1 Center, a cutting-edge arena that has become a centerpiece of downtown Sacramento. Alternatively, enjoy live performances at the historic Crest Theatre or the Sacramento Convention Center.

Annual Festivals and Events:

Sacramento's calendar is filled with lively festivals and events that celebrate the city's diverse culture and community spirit. Don't miss the colorful and energetic Sacramento Pride Parade and Festival, the lively Farm-to-Fork Festival, or the popular Gold Rush Days, where the streets of Old Sacramento come alive with reenactments and historical demonstrations. These events offer a chance to experience the vibrant energy and local traditions that define Sacramento.

Biking and Outdoor Activities:

With its flat terrain and extensive bike trail network, Sacramento is a cyclist's paradise. Rent a bike and explore the city's bike-friendly streets and scenic trails, such as the Jedediah Smith Memorial Trail that follows the American River. Additionally, enjoy boating on the Sacramento River, play a round of golf at one of the city's numerous courses, or simply relax in one of Sacramento's many parks and green spaces.

Craft Breweries and Wineries:

Sacramento's craft beer and wine scene has been flourishing in recent years. Explore the city's vibrant craft brewery scene, with breweries offering a wide range of unique and innovative brews. Take a short drive to nearby wineries in the Sacramento River Delta or the Clarksburg AVA, where you can sample award-winning wines and soak in the picturesque vineyard landscapes.

Sacramento seamlessly blends its rich history with a thriving modern culture, offering a vibrant and dynamic experience for visitors. Discover the city's historic landmarks, immerse yourself in its diverse neighborhoods, savor the farm-to-fork cuisine, and embrace the lively energy that defines Sacramento. Whether you're exploring its museums, enjoying outdoor activities, or simply soaking in the local charm, Sacramento will leave an indelible impression and invite you to return time and time again.

Lake Tahoe: A Year-Round Outdoor Playground

Welcome to Lake Tahoe, a breathtaking alpine oasis nestled in the Sierra Nevada Mountains of Northern California. Known for its crystal-clear waters, majestic mountains, and unparalleled natural beauty, Lake Tahoe offers a year-round outdoor playground for adventure enthusiasts and nature lovers alike. In this chapter, we will guide you through the wonders of Lake Tahoe, showcasing its scenic landscapes, thrilling recreational opportunities, and the remarkable experiences that make it a must-visit destination.

Pristine Alpine Beauty:

Lake Tahoe's pristine beauty is unparalleled. With its cobalt blue waters surrounded by snow-capped peaks, it's no wonder that this alpine lake is often referred to as the "Jewel of the Sierra." Take in the awe-inspiring vistas from one of the many scenic viewpoints along the lake, or embark on a boat cruise to fully immerse yourself in its enchanting ambiance.

Outdoor Recreation:

Lake Tahoe is a playground for outdoor enthusiasts, offering a wide range of recreational activities throughout the year. In the summer months, explore the lake's beaches and enjoy swimming, kayaking, paddleboarding, or simply basking in the sun. Hiking and mountain biking trails abound, catering to all skill levels and providing breathtaking views of the surrounding mountains. In the winter, Tahoe transforms into a winter wonderland, with world-class ski resorts offering downhill and cross-country skiing, snowboarding, snowshoeing, and even snowmobiling.

Heavenly Ski Resort:

Heavenly Ski Resort is a premier destination for winter sports enthusiasts. With its expansive terrain, breathtaking views of Lake Tahoe, and abundant snowfall, it offers an unforgettable skiing and snowboarding experience. The resort also features a vibrant village with shops, restaurants, and lively après-ski entertainment.

Emerald Bay State Park:

Visit Emerald Bay State Park, one of Lake Tahoe's most iconic and picturesque locations. Marvel at the deep azure waters and the stunning Fannette Island, the only island in Lake Tahoe. Explore the park's hiking trails, which offer panoramic views of the bay, or take a guided tour of the historic Vikingsholm Castle, a Scandinavian-inspired mansion nestled on the shore.

Sand Harbor:

Sand Harbor is a true gem of Lake Tahoe, known for its pristine sandy beaches and crystal-clear waters. Spend a day lounging on the beach, swimming in the refreshing waters, or picnicking amidst the breathtaking surroundings. During the summer, the Lake Tahoe Shakespeare Festival takes place at Sand Harbor, offering live theater performances in a stunning outdoor setting.

Tahoe Rim Trail:

For avid hikers and backpackers, the Tahoe Rim Trail is a must-visit. This 165-mile (265-kilometer) trail encircles the entire lake, offering stunning views, alpine meadows, and a chance to truly immerse yourself in the wilderness. Whether you choose to hike a short section or tackle the entire trail, the Tahoe Rim Trail provides an unforgettable adventure.

Water Sports and Recreation:

Lake Tahoe's crystal-clear waters are ideal for a variety of water sports and recreational activities. Rent a boat, kayak, or paddleboard to explore the lake at your own pace, or go on a guided fishing excursion to try your hand at catching trout or kokanee salmon. For the more adventurous, jet skiing, parasailing, and wakeboarding are popular choices.

Scenic Drives and Overlooks:

Lake Tahoe offers numerous scenic drives and overlooks that showcase its breathtaking beauty. Drive along the Lake Tahoe Scenic Byway, also known as Highway 89, which offers stunning vistas of the lake and access to several hiking trails and beaches. Don't miss the panoramic views from the Heavenly Gondola or the breathtaking overlooks at Mount Rose Summit and Spooner Summit.

Lake Tahoe Cruises:

Experience the beauty of Lake Tahoe from a

different perspective by taking a scenic cruise. Board one of the many cruise boats that traverse the lake, offering stunning views of the surrounding mountains and shoreline. Some cruises even provide narration about the lake's history, geology, and wildlife, enhancing your understanding and appreciation of this natural wonder.

Golfing:

Lake Tahoe is home to several world-class golf courses that offer breathtaking views and challenging fairways. Tee off amidst the mountain backdrop and pristine landscapes, and enjoy a round of golf in this stunning alpine setting. Whether you're a seasoned golfer or a beginner, the golf courses of Lake Tahoe provide a memorable experience for players of all levels.

Winter Wonderland:

During the winter months, Lake Tahoe transforms into a winter wonderland. The region's ski resorts, including Squaw Valley, Northstar California, and Kirkwood Mountain Resort, offer world-class skiing and snowboarding opportunities. Experience the thrill of gliding down the slopes, surrounded by stunning mountain vistas and fresh, powdery snow.

Year-Round Festivals and Events:

Lake Tahoe hosts a variety of festivals and events throughout the year, adding to its vibrant cultural scene. From the annual Lake Tahoe Shakespeare Festival to the Lake Tahoe Music

Festival and the Valhalla Art, Music, and Theatre Festival, there's always something happening to entertain and delight visitors. These events provide a unique opportunity to experience the arts, music, and culture against the backdrop of Lake Tahoe's natural beauty.

Lake Tahoe's allure as a year-round outdoor playground is undeniable. Its pristine waters, majestic mountains, and endless recreational opportunities make it a destination that will leave a lasting impression. Whether you're skiing down the slopes in winter, hiking the scenic trails in summer, or simply basking in the beauty of the lake, Lake Tahoe invites you to embrace the wonders of nature and create memories that will be cherished for a lifetime. Immerse yourself in the breathtaking landscapes, embark on thrilling adventures, and savor the tranquility of this alpine paradise.

Silicon Valley: Exploring Tech Innovation

Welcome to Silicon Valley, the global hub of technology and innovation, nestled in the heart of Northern California. Home to some of the world's most influential tech companies, Silicon Valley offers a unique opportunity to explore the cutting-edge advancements that are shaping our future. In this chapter, we will guide you through the essence of Silicon Valley, showcasing its iconic tech landmarks, startup culture, entrepreneurial spirit, and the remarkable experiences that make it a must-visit destination for tech enthusiasts and curious travelers alike.

The Birthplace of Tech Giants:

Silicon Valley is renowned for being the birthplace of tech giants that have revolutionized the world. Pay homage to the roots of this technological revolution by visiting the Garage in Palo Alto, where Hewlett-Packard was founded. Explore the iconic Stanford University campus, which has played a crucial role in fostering innovation and entrepreneurship. Delve into the history of Silicon Valley and gain insight into the ideas and inventions that have shaped our digital era.

Tech Company Headquarters:

Silicon Valley is home to the headquarters of many renowned tech companies. Take a tour of the Googleplex in Mountain View, where you can explore the campus and learn about the company's innovative projects. Visit the Apple Park Visitor

Center in Cupertino, where you can immerse yourself in the Apple ecosystem and marvel at the state-of-the-art architecture. Don't miss the Facebook campus in Menlo Park, where you can discover the social media giant's latest developments and initiatives.

Tech Museums and Exhibits:

Immerse yourself in the world of technology by visiting the tech museums and exhibits scattered throughout Silicon Valley. The Computer History Museum in Mountain View offers a fascinating journey through the history of computing, showcasing vintage computers, interactive exhibits, and a comprehensive collection of artifacts. The Tech Interactive in San Jose provides hands-on exhibits that allow visitors to explore the realms of robotics, virtual reality, and artificial intelligence.

Stanford Research Park:

Venture into the Stanford Research Park, a sprawling campus that serves as a hub for innovation and collaboration. Discover the groundbreaking research being conducted by startups, established companies, and Stanford University itself. Attend lectures, workshops, and events that showcase the latest advancements in various fields, from biotechnology to artificial intelligence.

Startup Culture and Incubators:

Silicon Valley's startup culture is renowned worldwide. Visit startup incubators and accelerators, such as Y Combinator or Plug and Play Tech Center, where you can witness the birth of groundbreaking ideas and connect with the entrepreneurs driving innovation. Attend startup pitch events and networking sessions to gain insight into the entrepreneurial ecosystem and witness the energy and creativity that permeate the region.

Tech Meetups and Conferences:

Silicon Valley hosts a plethora of tech meetups, conferences, and workshops throughout the year. Attend these events to network with industry professionals, hear from thought leaders, and gain knowledge about the latest trends and advancements in various fields. Whether it's a tech conference focused on artificial intelligence, blockchain, or clean energy, these gatherings provide a platform for learning, collaboration, and inspiration.

Venture Capital and Investment:

Silicon Valley is synonymous with venture capital and investment. Explore the venture capital firms that fuel the region's innovation, and gain insight into the process of funding and supporting startups. Attend pitch events or startup showcases to witness entrepreneurs pitching their ideas to potential investors, and learn about the ecosystem that drives the growth and success of Silicon Valley startups.

Tech Entrepreneurship:

Silicon Valley's entrepreneurial spirit is

infectious, inspiring individuals from around the world to pursue their startup dreams. Dive into the world of tech entrepreneurship by attending startup boot camps or entrepreneurship programs offered by universities and incubators. Connect with like-minded individuals, share ideas, and learn from successful entrepreneurs who have navigated thechallenges and triumphs of building their own companies.

Innovation Centers and Labs:

Silicon Valley is home to numerous innovation centers and labs where groundbreaking research and development take place. Visit the Xerox PARC (Palo Alto Research Center), where many fundamental technologies of the digital era were invented, including the graphical user interface and Ethernet. Explore innovation hubs like the NASA Ames Research Center or the Lawrence Livermore National Laboratory, where scientists and engineers push the boundaries of knowledge and technology.

Tech-Driven Attractions:

Beyond the corporate campuses and research centers, Silicon Valley offers a range of tech-driven attractions for visitors. Experience the thrill of virtual reality at a VR arcade, or test your coding skills at an escape room with a tech twist. Visit futuristic robotic labs or attend drone demonstrations that showcase the latest advancements in robotics and automation.

Outdoor Recreation and Natural Beauty:

While Silicon Valley is synonymous with technology, it is also surrounded by stunning natural beauty. Take a break from the tech world and explore the region's outdoor recreation areas. Enjoy hiking, biking, or picnicking in the Santa Cruz Mountains or venture to nearby parks like Henry W. Coe State Park or Rancho San Antonio Preserve. Embrace the balance between innovation and nature that makes Silicon Valley truly unique.

Culinary Delights and Cultural Diversity:

Silicon Valley's vibrant culinary scene reflects its diverse population and international influences. Sample global cuisines at food trucks, pop-up restaurants, or ethnic eateries that line the streets. Visit local farmers' markets to savor farm-to-table produce and artisanal products. Explore cultural festivals and events that celebrate the diversity of Silicon Valley's population, providing an opportunity to experience different traditions, music, and cuisine.

Silicon Valley is a testament to the power of human ingenuity and innovation. It is a place where ideas become reality, and where technology continues to shape our world. Embrace the spirit of exploration and discovery as you delve into the tech culture, visit iconic company headquarters, and engage with the entrepreneurs and visionaries who are driving the future. Silicon Valley invites you to be inspired, to dream big, and to witness firsthand the transformative power of technology.

Gold Country: Tracing California's Rich History

Welcome to Gold Country, a region in Northern California steeped in history and known for its significant role in the California Gold Rush of the mid-19th century. Journey back in time as you explore the towns, museums, and landmarks that bear witness to this transformative era. In this chapter, we will guide you through the essence of Gold Country, tracing California's rich history and showcasing the remarkable experiences that make it a captivating destination for history enthusiasts and curious travelers.

The California Gold Rush:

Gold Country was at the heart of the California Gold Rush, which began in 1848 when gold was discovered at Sutter's Mill in Coloma. Learn about this pivotal event in American history, as droves of fortune seekers flocked to the region in search of gold. Explore the Marshall Gold Discovery State Historic Park in Coloma, where you can visit the site of the original gold discovery and learn about the lives of the miners through exhibits and guided tours.

Historic Towns:

Gold Country is dotted with charming historic towns that have preserved their Gold Rush-era architecture and ambiance. Visit Placerville, also known as "Hangtown," where you can stroll through the historic Main Street lined with quaint shops and restaurants. Explore Nevada City and

Grass Valley, both with well-preserved downtown areas showcasing Victorian architecture and vibrant cultural scenes. These towns offer a glimpse into the past and provide a sense of the region's rich history.

Museums and Interpretive Centers:

Delve deeper into the history of Gold Country by visiting the numerous museums and interpretive centers that document the Gold Rush era. The California State Mining and Mineral Museum in Mariposa showcases a collection of gold and mineral specimens, as well as artifacts from the Gold Rush. The Gold Rush Museum in Auburn and the Placer County Museum in Roseville provide exhibits and interactive displays that bring the Gold Rush era to life.

Gold Panning and Mining Experiences:

Experience the excitement of gold panning and mining firsthand by participating in guided tours and hands-on experiences. Join a gold panning demonstration and try your luck in the rivers and streams that still yield small amounts of gold today. Learn about traditional mining techniques, visit mine sites, and gain insight into the arduous lives of the miners who toiled in the pursuit of gold.

Historic Landmarks and Sites:

Gold Country is replete with historic landmarks and sites that serve as reminders of the region's storied past. Visit Columbia State Historic Park, a preserved Gold Rush town where you can walk the streets as they appeared in the 19th century, interact with costumed guides, and witness live demonstrations of traditional crafts. Explore the Kennedy Gold Mine in Jackson, one of the deepest gold mines in the world, and take a guided underground tour to learn about the mining operations.

Railroads and Transportation History:

Discover the role of railroads in shaping the history of Gold Country. Visit the California State Railroad Museum in Sacramento, where you can explore historic locomotives and learn about the vital role of railroads during the Gold Rush. Take a ride on a historic steam train at Railtown 1897 State Historic Park in Jamestown, experiencing the nostalgia of a bygone era.

Wine Tasting and Vineyards:

Gold Country is not only known for its rich history but also for its flourishing wine industry. Explore the region's vineyards and wineries, where you can sample award-winning wines and learn about the winemaking process. The Sierra Foothills AVA, which encompasses Gold Country, is renowned for its diverse range of grape varieties and terroir. Enjoy scenic vineyard views, attend wine festivals, and indulge in the culinary delights that accompany the wine tasting experience.

Outdoor Recreation:

GoldCountry's natural beauty provides ample opportunities for outdoor recreation. Explore the scenic landscapes through hiking and biking trails that wind through the foothills and mountain ranges. Enjoy fishing or boating on the region's lakes and rivers, or go camping amidst the tranquil surroundings. Embrace the serenity of nature as you immerse yourself in the same landscapes that captivated the early pioneers during the Gold Rush.

Ghost Towns and Mining Camps:

Discover the remnants of ghost towns and mining camps that were once bustling centers during the Gold Rush. Explore Bodie State Historic Park, a preserved ghost town that offers a glimpse into the lives of the miners and their families. Walk the deserted streets and peer into the preserved buildings, witnessing the stark contrast between past and present.

Cultural Events and Festivals:

Gold Country celebrates its history and heritage through a variety of cultural events and festivals. Attend living history events, where reenactors recreate scenes from the Gold Rush era, bringing the past to life. Experience pioneer crafts, music, and dance at events like the Nevada City Victorian Christmas or the Calaveras County Fair and Jumping Frog Jubilee. These festivities provide a lively and immersive experience that transports visitors back in time.

Scenic Drives and Panoramic Views:

Gold Country boasts numerous scenic drives that showcase its picturesque landscapes and panoramic views. Travel along the historic

Highway 49, named after the "49ers" who came in search of gold, to experience the region's rich history and stunning vistas. Don't miss the breathtaking views from overlooks such as Inspiration Point in Auburn or Daffodil Hill in Volcano, where fields of vibrant daffodils blanket the landscape in spring.

Culinary Heritage and Local Flavors:

Gold Country's culinary scene reflects its rich history and agricultural heritage. Savor farm-to-table cuisine featuring locally sourced ingredients, and sample the flavors of the region at farmers' markets and roadside stands. Taste traditional dishes that pay homage to the Gold Rush era, such as hearty stews, sourdough bread, and apple pie made with Gold Country's renowned apples.

Gold Country invites you to immerse yourself in the rich tapestry of California's history. From the excitement of the Gold Rush to the preservation of historic towns and landmarks, this region offers a glimpse into the past while providing a vibrant and engaging present. Explore the museums, mine sites, and cultural events, and let the stories of the pioneers and their quest for gold inspire your own sense of adventure and discovery. Trace California's rich history in Gold Country and create lasting memories rooted in the triumphs and challenges of a bygone era.

Mendocino County: A Charming Coastal Escape

Welcome to Mendocino County, a picturesque coastal escape nestled along the rugged northern California coastline. Known for its breathtaking scenery, charming coastal towns, and vibrant arts scene, Mendocino County offers a tranquil retreat for nature lovers, wine enthusiasts, and those seeking a slower pace of life. In this chapter, we will guide you through the essence of Mendocino County, showcasing its natural beauty, cultural treasures, and the remarkable experiences that make it a must-visit destination for travelers.

Mendocino Village:

Begin your exploration of Mendocino County in the town of Mendocino itself. This historic village is a delight to explore, with its Victorian-era buildings, quaint shops, and stunning ocean views. Stroll along the streets lined with art galleries, boutiques, and charming cafes. Don't miss the Ford House Visitor Center, where you can learn about the town's history and pick up information about local attractions.

Mendocino Headlands State Park:

Discover the natural beauty of the Mendocino Headlands State Park, which encompasses the rugged coastline surrounding the town of Mendocino. Explore the network of trails that wind along the cliffs, offering panoramic views of the Pacific Ocean and glimpses of wildlife such as seabirds and harbor seals. Take in the dramatic scenery and enjoy the serenity of this coastal paradise.

Mendocino Coast Botanical Gardens:

Immerse yourself in the beauty of nature at the Mendocino Coast Botanical Gardens. This expansive garden showcases a diverse collection of plant species, including stunning displays of rhododendrons, dahlias, and succulents. Take a leisurely stroll through the manicured gardens, explore the coastal trails, and appreciate the harmonious blend of native flora and horticultural wonders.

Point Cabrillo Light Station:

Visit the Point Cabrillo Light Station, a historic lighthouse perched atop a rocky promontory near Mendocino. Learn about the fascinating maritime history of the region and climb to the top of the lighthouse for breathtaking views of the rugged coastline. Take a leisurely walk along the surrounding trails and revel in the natural beauty that surrounds this iconic landmark.

Wine Tasting in Anderson Valley:

Mendocino County is renowned for its wine production, and a visit to Anderson Valley is a must for wine enthusiasts. Discover boutique wineries nestled amidst rolling vineyards, where you can savor award-winning wines in a serene and unpretentious setting. Sample the region's acclaimed Pinot Noir, Chardonnay, and sparkling wines while enjoying the scenic beauty of the valley.

Redwood Forests:

Mendocino County is home to magnificent old-growth redwood forests that inspire a sense of awe and reverence. Explore Montgomery Woods State Natural Reserve, where you can walk amidst towering redwoods and experience the tranquil ambiance of these ancient giants. Hike along the shaded trails, listen to the gentle rustling of leaves, and allow the serenity of the forest to envelop you.

Russian Gulch State Park:

Venture to Russian Gulch State Park, a coastal park that offers a diverse range of natural attractions. Explore the park's lush forests, picturesque waterfalls, and scenic coastal bluffs. Hike the trails that lead to the Devil's Punchbowl, a collapsed sea cave, and witness the power of the Pacific Ocean as waves crash against the rocky shoreline.

Mendocino Coast Scenic Drive:

Embark on a scenic drive along the Mendocino Coast, where you'll be treated to breathtaking vistas at every turn. The winding coastal Highway 1 takes you through picturesque towns, along towering cliffs, and past secluded beaches. Stop at pullouts along the wayto take in the panoramic views, snap photos of the rugged coastline, and breathe in the fresh ocean air. Enjoy the serenity of the open road as you immerse yourself in the natural beauty of the Mendocino coastline.

Arts and Culture:

Mendocino County boasts a vibrant arts scene that is sure to captivate creative souls. Explore the numerous art galleries and studios that showcase the works of local artists, ranging from paintings and sculptures to ceramics and jewelry. Attend art openings and exhibitions, where you can meet the artists and gain insight into their creative process. Immerse yourself in the cultural richness of the region through performances at local theaters, musical concerts, and lively community events.

Mendocino County Farmers' Markets:

Experience the bountiful flavors of Mendocino County at its farmers' markets. These vibrant gatherings showcase the region's agricultural abundance, featuring an array of fresh produce, artisanal products, and local crafts. Engage with the farmers and artisans, sample seasonal fruits, and discover the culinary treasures that define the farm-to-table culture of the county.

Mendocino County Mushroom Forays:

Mendocino County is known for its abundant and diverse mushroom species. Join a guided mushroom foray led by knowledgeable experts who will introduce you to the fascinating world of fungi. Learn about different mushroom species, their habitats, and the art of foraging. Discover the joy of uncovering hidden treasures in the forest as you search for edible mushrooms.

Coastal Cuisine and Farm-to-Table Delights:

Indulge in the culinary delights of Mendocino County, where coastal cuisine meets farm-to-table freshness. Savor locally caught seafood, such as Dungeness crab and Pacific salmon, prepared with innovative flair. Enjoy farm-fresh ingredients in gourmet dishes at the county's top-notch restaurants. Immerse yourself in the culinary scene by participating in food and wine festivals that celebrate the region's flavors and the talents of its chefs.

Mendocino County invites you to escape to a charming coastal haven, where natural beauty, cultural treasures, and a sense of tranquility converge. Discover the allure of picturesque towns, immerse yourself in the artistic and culinary delights, and reconnect with nature along the scenic coastline. Mendocino County is a destination that will rejuvenate your spirit, nourish your soul, and leave you with cherished memories of a truly unforgettable experience.

Monterey and Carmel: Coastal Beauty and Marine Wonders

Welcome to Monterey and Carmel, two enchanting coastal towns located along the breathtaking central California coastline. Known for their natural beauty, rich history, and diverse marine life, Monterey and Carmel offer a captivating blend of coastal charm and marine wonders. In this chapter, we will guide you through the essence of these coastal gems, showcasing their scenic landscapes, iconic attractions, and the remarkable experiences that make them must-visit destinations for travelers.

Cannery Row:

Begin your exploration in Monterey by visiting Cannery Row, a vibrant waterfront district with a storied past. Once home to bustling sardine canneries, Cannery Row has been transformed into a lively area filled with shops, restaurants, and attractions. Explore the historic buildings that have been repurposed into boutique hotels and galleries, or visit the Monterey Bay Aquarium, one of the world's premier marine research and conservation institutions.

Monterey Bay Aquarium:

A visit to Monterey would not be complete without experiencing the Monterey Bay Aquarium. Located on the iconic Cannery Row, this world-class aquarium showcases a stunning array of marine life, including playful sea otters, mesmerizing jellyfish, and graceful sea turtles.

Explore the interactive exhibits, learn about the diverse ecosystems of the Monterey Bay, and witness the aquarium's commitment to marine conservation.

Point Lobos State Natural Reserve:

Venture south of Carmel to Point Lobos State Natural Reserve, often referred to as the "crown jewel" of the California State Park system. This protected coastal reserve offers breathtaking views, rugged cliffs, and diverse wildlife. Hike along the scenic trails that wind through cypress groves and rocky shoreline, keeping an eye out for sea lions, harbor seals, and various bird species. The dramatic landscapes and serene ambiance make Point Lobos a haven for nature lovers and photographers.

17-Mile Drive:

Embark on the iconic 17-Mile Drive, a scenic coastal road that winds through Pebble Beach and Pacific Grove, offering unparalleled vistas of the Pacific Ocean and stunning landscapes. Along the drive, you'll encounter famous landmarks such as the Lone Cypress, Bird Rock, and the enchanting Del Monte Forest. Stop at designated viewpoints to capture the beauty of the coastline and take in the fresh ocean breeze.

Pebble Beach Golf Links:

Golf enthusiasts should not miss the opportunity to visit Pebble Beach Golf Links, one of the most prestigious golf courses in the world. This stunning course is situated along the rugged coastline and offers breathtaking views of the Pacific Ocean. Even if you're not a golfer, a visit to the clubhouse or a stroll along the coastal paths surrounding the course provides a taste of the beauty and elegance that Pebble Beach is known for.

Historic Monterey:

Delve into the rich history of Monterey by exploring its historic landmarks and neighborhoods. Visit the Monterey State Historic Park, a collection of adobe buildings that preserve the city's Spanish and Mexican heritage. Explore the Custom House, California's first customhouse and now a museum, to learn about Monterey's role as the capital of Spanish and Mexican California. Stroll through the streets of Old Monterey, admiring the well-preserved architecture and discovering charming shops and restaurants.

Pacific Grove:

Adjacent to Monterey lies the charming town of Pacific Grove, known for its Victorian-era architecture and scenic coastline. Explore the picturesque downtown area, filled with quaint shops and bed-and-breakfasts. Visit the Pacific Grove Museum of Natural History to learn about the region's flora, fauna, and geological history. Take a leisurely walk along the Pacific Grove shoreline, known as Lover's Point, and watch the mesmerizing waves crash against the rocky coastline.

Carmel-by-the-Sea:

Venture south to Carmel-by-the-Sea, a quaint and artistic town that exudes a romantic and bohemian charm. Meander through the charming streets lined with art galleries, boutiques, and cafes. Admire the fairytale-like cottages and secret gardens that add to the town's enchanting ambiance. Take a stroll along Carmel Beach, known for its pristine white sands and stunning sunsets. Carmel-by-the-Sea's artistic spirit is further exemplified by its numerous art galleries and the renowned Sunset Center, a venue for performing arts and cultural events.

Carmel Mission:

Immerse yourself in history by visiting the Carmel Mission, also known as Mission San Carlos Borromeo del Río Carmelo. This historic mission, founded in 1770, is one of the most beautiful and well-preserved in California. Explore the mission grounds, visit the basilica, and learn about the mission's role in shaping the history and culture of the region. The peaceful gardens and serene atmosphere create a tranquil retreat within the heart of Carmel.

Scenic Ocean Drive:

Experience the stunning beauty of the central California coastline by taking a scenic drive along the Ocean Drive. This picturesque route follows Highway 1, offering breathtaking views of the rugged cliffs, crashing waves, and coastal vistas. Stop at scenic viewpoints, such as Bixby Bridge and Rocky Point, to capture the dramatic landscapes and appreciate the raw power of the Pacific Ocean.

Whale Watching:

Mendocino and Carmel are both renowned for their excellent whale-watching opportunities. Join a whale-watching excursion to witness the majestic beauty of whales as they migrate along the coast. Gray whales, humpback whales, and even orcas can often be spotted during the migration seasons. Embark on a thrilling adventure that connects you with the marine wonders of the Monterey Bay.

Coastal Cuisine:

Indulge in the culinary delights of Monterey and Carmel, where fresh seafood and farm-to-table ingredients take center stage. Sample delectable dishes at renowned seafood restaurants, or dine at cozy bistros that offer a fusion of international flavors. Explore the local farmers' markets to savor the abundance of seasonal produce, artisanal cheeses, and regional specialties. The coastal setting adds a touch of magic to the dining experience, allowing you to savor the flavors while enjoying the stunning views of the Pacific Ocean.

Monterey and Carmel invite you to immerse yourself in their coastal beauty, rich history, and marine wonders. Explore iconic attractions, embrace the artistic and bohemian spirit, and witness the incredible marine life that thrives in the Monterey Bay. Discover the charm of these coastal towns, where natural beauty meets cultural treasures, and create lasting memories of a truly enchanting coastal getaway.

Yosemite National Park: A Natural Wonderland

Welcome to Yosemite National Park, a pristine and awe-inspiring natural wonder located in the heart of the Sierra Nevada Mountains of Northern California. Known for its towering granite cliffs, cascading waterfalls, ancient giant sequoias, and diverse wildlife, Yosemite is a sanctuary of breathtaking beauty and a paradise for outdoor enthusiasts and nature lovers. In this chapter, we will guide you through the essence of Yosemite National Park, showcasing its iconic landmarks, awe-inspiring landscapes, and the remarkable experiences that make it a must-visit destination for travelers.

Yosemite Valley:

Begin your journey in Yosemite Valley, the crown jewel of the park and the epicenter of its natural wonders. Marvel at the towering granite cliffs, including the iconic El Capitan and Half Dome, which dominate the valley's skyline. Take in the panoramic views from Tunnel View, a viewpoint that offers a breathtaking vista of Yosemite Valley, El Capitan, Bridalveil Fall, and the distant Yosemite Falls. Explore the valley floor, where you can hike, bike, or simply enjoy a leisurely stroll while soaking in the magnificent scenery.

Waterfalls:

Yosemite National Park is renowned for its spectacular waterfalls, which cascade down the granite cliffs with thundering force. Witness the power and beauty of Yosemite Falls, one of the tallest waterfalls in North America, as it plunges into the valley below. Visit Bridalveil Fall, known for its delicate and misty appearance, or hike to the base of Vernal Fall and Nevada Fall along the Mist Trail, immersing yourself in the spray and thunder of these breathtaking cascades.

Giant Sequoias:

Venture to Mariposa Grove, a grove of ancient giant sequoia trees that have stood tall for thousands of years. Marvel at the sheer size and grandeur of these magnificent giants, including the famous Grizzly Giant and the California Tunnel Tree. Take a leisurely walk along the trails that wind through the grove, allowing you to connect with the serenity and majesty of these ancient sentinels.

Glacier Point:

Embark on a journey to Glacier Point, a viewpoint perched on the edge of a sheer granite cliff, offering sweeping vistas of Yosemite Valley, Half Dome, and the surrounding high country. Take in the breathtaking panoramic views, especially during sunset or sunrise when the changing light paints the landscape in vibrant hues. It's also a popular spot for stargazing, as the dark skies of Yosemite provide a stunning backdrop for celestial wonders.

Tuolumne Meadows:

Venture into the high country of Yosemite to

explore Tuolumne Meadows, a vast alpine meadow surrounded by majestic peaks and granite domes. Hike along the meandering Tuolumne River, breathe in the crisp mountain air, and witness the wildflowers that blanket the meadows in a riot of colors during the summer months. Experience the tranquility of this high-altitude paradise and connect with the unspoiled beauty of the Sierra Nevada.

Hiking and Backpacking:

Yosemite offers an extensive network of hiking trails, catering to all levels of fitness and experience. From easy nature walks to challenging multi-day backpacking trips, there is a trail for every adventurer. Embark on the iconic hike to the top of Half Dome, using cables to ascend the final stretch and be rewarded with breathtaking views from the summit. Explore the Mist Trail, which takes you past Vernal Fall and Nevada Fall, or venture into the backcountry on the John Muir Trail or the Pacific Crest Trail.

Rock Climbing:

Yosemite is a mecca for rock climbers, attracting enthusiasts from around the world. The park offers a multitude of granite cliffs and domes that provide a diverse range of climbing experiences,from beginner-friendly routes to challenging climbs for seasoned professionals. Test your skills on the iconic granite faces of El Capitan or Sentinel Rock, or try your hand at bouldering in the legendary Camp 4. Whether you're a novice climber or a seasoned expert, Yosemite offers endless opportunities to push your limits and experience the thrill of scaling vertical walls in a breathtaking natural setting.

Wildlife:

Yosemite is home to a diverse array of wildlife, including black bears, deer, coyotes, bobcats, and a variety of bird species. Keep your eyes peeled for these magnificent creatures as you explore the park. Join a ranger-led wildlife viewing program to learn about the park's ecological balance and the efforts to protect its inhabitants. Remember to practice responsible wildlife viewing and maintain a safe distance to ensure the well-being of both the animals and yourself.

Photography:

Yosemite's breathtaking landscapes and iconic landmarks provide endless opportunities for photography enthusiasts. Capture the ethereal beauty of sunrise or sunset reflecting on the granite cliffs, or photograph the play of light and shadows in the valley. Visit during the spring when the waterfalls are at their peak, or in the fall when the colors of the foliage create a tapestry of vibrant hues. Allow the natural beauty of Yosemite to ignite your creativity and capture moments that will be cherished for a lifetime.

Camping and Stargazing:

Immerse yourself in the tranquility of Yosemite's wilderness by camping under the starry night sky. The park offers several campgrounds, from developed sites with amenities to more primitive options for those seeking a back-to-nature experience. Set up camp amidst the towering trees, enjoy campfire conversations, and witness the brilliance of the night sky as you gaze at the countless stars twinkling above.

Ranger Programs and Interpretive Centers:

Take advantage of the ranger-led programs and interpretive centers scattered throughout the park. Join a guided hike, attend a nature talk, or participate in a stargazing event to deepen your understanding of Yosemite's natural and cultural history. Visit the Yosemite Valley Visitor Center or the Tuolumne Meadows Visitor Center, where exhibits, displays, and knowledgeable rangers provide insights into the park's geology, wildlife, and conservation efforts.

Cultural Heritage:

Yosemite has a rich cultural heritage that is deeply intertwined with the history of Native American tribes and early explorers. Learn about the indigenous peoples who have called this land home for thousands of years and gain appreciation for their deep connection to the natural world. Visit the Yosemite Museum in Yosemite Valley, which showcases the cultural artifacts and traditions of the Miwok and Paiute tribes. Engage in conversations and events that celebrate the diversity of the park's cultural heritage and foster understanding and respect for all who cherish this natural wonder.

Yosemite National Park is a sanctuary of natural beauty and a testament to the power and wonder of the natural world. Whether you seek adventure, serenity, or simply a deep appreciation for the grandeur of nature, Yosemite invites you to explore its majestic landscapes, connect with its diverse ecosystems, and create memories that will last a lifetime. Let the magic of Yosemite unfold before your eyes and ignite your spirit of adventure and exploration.

Exploring the Sierra Nevada Mountains

Welcome to the Sierra Nevada Mountains, a majestic range that spans across eastern California and offers a wealth of natural beauty, outdoor adventures, and diverse ecosystems. From towering peaks and alpine meadows to crystal-clear lakes and ancient forests, the Sierra Nevada Mountains are a paradise for outdoor enthusiasts, hikers, and nature lovers. In this chapter, we will guide you through the essence of the Sierra Nevada Mountains, showcasing its stunning landscapes, iconic destinations, and the remarkable experiences that make it a must-explore region for travelers.

An Introduction to the Sierra Nevada Mountains:

Begin your journey by familiarizing yourself with the grandeur and significance of the Sierra Nevada Mountains. Discover the geological history and formation of this magnificent range, which stretches over 400 miles and includes some of the highest peaks in the contiguous United States. Learn about the diverse ecosystems that thrive within its boundaries, from alpine tundra to lush forests, and understand the role the mountains play in providing water resources for the surrounding regions.

Yosemite National Park:

No exploration of the Sierra Nevada Mountains would be complete without a visit to Yosemite National Park, a crown jewel of natural wonders. Marvel at the towering granite cliffs, thundering waterfalls, and ancient sequoia groves. Embark on hikes to iconic landmarks like Half Dome and Glacier Point, or simply immerse yourself in the tranquil beauty of Yosemite Valley. Discover the unique ecosystems and breathtaking landscapes that have captivated visitors for generations.

Lake Tahoe:

Journey to Lake Tahoe, a shimmering alpine lake nestled amidst the Sierra Nevada Mountains. Experience the pristine beauty of its crystal-clear waters, framed by majestic peaks. Enjoy a variety of recreational activities, from swimming and boating in the summer to skiing and snowboarding in the winter. Explore the surrounding trails, which offer stunning views of the lake and the opportunity to connect with the natural splendor of the region.

Sequoia and Kings Canyon National Parks:

Venture south to Sequoia and Kings Canyon National Parks, home to the world's largest trees and stunning mountain vistas. Stand in awe beneath the towering giants of the Giant Forest, including the legendary General Sherman Tree, believed to be the largest living tree on Earth. Hike through alpine meadows, explore deep canyons, and witness the dramatic landscapes that make these parks a treasure trove of natural wonders.

Alpine Lakes and Wilderness Areas:

Discover the numerous alpine lakes and

wilderness areas that dot the Sierra Nevada Mountains. From the pristine waters of Desolation Wilderness to the tranquil beauty of the John Muir Wilderness, these remote and unspoiled landscapes offer a haven for outdoor adventurers. Hike to glacial lakes such as Lake Aloha or Thousand Island Lake, and savor the serenity and solitude that can only be found in the heart of the mountains.

Mammoth Lakes:

Visit the picturesque town of Mammoth Lakes, nestled in the Eastern Sierra region. Known for its world-class skiing and snowboarding in winter, Mammoth Lakes offers year-round outdoor activities. In the summer, explore the stunning landscapes of the Mammoth Lakes Basin, hike to hidden waterfalls, or try your hand at fishing in the crystal-clear alpine lakes. The town itself offers a charming alpine atmosphere with cozy lodges, gourmet restaurants, and a vibrant arts scene.

Outdoor Adventures:

The Sierra Nevada Mountains provide endless opportunities for outdoor adventures. Embark on backpacking trips along the legendary Pacific Crest Trail, test your rock climbing skills on the granite cliffs of Lover's Leap, or go whitewater rafting on the thrilling rapids of the American River. The region is a playground for outdoor enthusiasts, offering activities such as mountain biking, horseback riding, fishing, and birdwatching. Let the mountains igniteyour sense of adventure and immerse yourself in the exhilarating experiences that await.

Hot Springs and Natural Wonders:

Unwind and rejuvenate in the natural hot springs that can be found throughout the Sierra Nevada Mountains. Relax in the warm, mineral-rich waters as you soak in the tranquility of the surrounding landscapes. Visit unique geological formations such as Mono Lake, with its mesmerizing tufa towers, or explore hidden gems like Alabama Hills, a stunning rock formation that has served as a backdrop for numerous films.

Historic Towns and Cultural Heritage:

The Sierra Nevada Mountains are steeped in history and cultural heritage. Explore the historic mining towns that sprung up during the Gold Rush era, such as Nevada City and Placerville, where you can immerse yourself in the nostalgia of the past. Visit the Manzanar National Historic Site, which commemorates the internment of Japanese Americans during World War II and provides insight into this dark chapter of American history. Engage with the local communities, attend festivals and events, and learn about the diverse cultural tapestry that weaves through the region.

Scenic Drives:

Embark on scenic drives that wind through the Sierra Nevada Mountains, offering breathtaking vistas and access to hidden gems. Travel the Tioga Road in Yosemite National Park, which takes you through high alpine meadows and offers stunning views of the surrounding peaks. Drive the Sonora Pass Scenic Byway, a winding mountain road that offers breathtaking views of the Eastern Sierra and takes you through charming towns and historic sites.

Wildlife Viewing:

The Sierra Nevada Mountains are home to a rich variety of wildlife, including black bears, mountain lions, mule deer, and a plethora of bird species. Keep your eyes peeled for these magnificent creatures as you explore the mountains. Visit wildlife sanctuaries and nature preserves, or simply take a hike through the wilderness to catch a glimpse of the diverse fauna that inhabits this pristine environment.

Conservation and Stewardship:

As you explore the Sierra Nevada Mountains, it is important to remember the significance of conservation and stewardship. Understand the delicate balance of the ecosystems and the challenges they face due to climate change and human impact. Practice Leave No Trace principles, respect wildlife and their habitats, and support local organizations and initiatives dedicated to preserving the natural beauty and ecological integrity of the Sierra Nevada Mountains.

The Sierra Nevada Mountains are a treasure trove of natural wonders, offering a playground for outdoor adventures and a sanctuary for those seeking solace in nature's embrace. Immerse yourself in the grandeur of towering peaks, crystal-clear lakes, and ancient forests. Let the mountains inspire your sense of exploration, ignite your spirit of adventure, and leave you with cherished memories of a truly transformative journey through this remarkable region.

Santa Cruz: Surf, Sun, and Beach Vibes

Welcome to Santa Cruz, a vibrant coastal city located on the northern edge of Monterey Bay. Known for its world-class surf breaks, sandy beaches, and laid-back atmosphere, Santa Cruz offers the perfect blend of surf culture, outdoor adventures, and beachfront relaxation. In this chapter, we will guide you through the essence of Santa Cruz, showcasing its iconic beaches, thriving surf scene, and the remarkable experiences that make it a must-visit destination for travelers.

Santa Cruz Beach Boardwalk:

Begin your Santa Cruz adventure at the iconic Santa Cruz Beach Boardwalk, a seaside amusement park that has been delighting visitors since 1907. Experience the thrill of classic rides, such as the Giant Dipper wooden roller coaster and the Looff Carousel, or test your skills at the arcade games. Enjoy a leisurely stroll along the boardwalk, indulge in delicious carnival treats, and soak up the lively atmosphere that makes this historic landmark a favorite among visitors and locals alike.

Surfing Culture:

Immerse yourself in the vibrant surf culture that defines Santa Cruz. Known as the "Surf City," Santa Cruz boasts world-class surf breaks that attract surfers from around the globe. Whether you're a seasoned pro or a beginner looking to catch your first wave, there are surf spots for every skill level. Head to renowned surf breaks like

Steamer Lane, Pleasure Point, or Cowell's Beach to witness the skilled surfers in action or take a surf lesson to experience the thrill of riding the waves yourself.

Natural Bridges State Beach:

Visit Natural Bridges State Beach, a picturesque coastal park named after its iconic natural rock bridge formation. Explore the sandy shores, walk along the scenic trails, and marvel at the coastal cliffs that surround the beach. During the winter months, the beach becomes a gathering spot for migrating monarch butterflies, offering a unique opportunity to witness the awe-inspiring spectacle of thousands of butterflies clustering together.

West Cliff Drive:

Take a leisurely drive or bike ride along West Cliff Drive, a scenic coastal road that offers breathtaking views of the Pacific Ocean and the Santa Cruz coastline. Admire the surfers riding the waves at Steamer Lane, enjoy the panoramic vistas from the cliffside overlooks, and stop at Lighthouse Point to explore the Santa Cruz Surfing Museum. The drive along West Cliff Drive allows you to soak in the beauty of the ocean and the charming beachfront neighborhoods.

Beaches:

Santa Cruz is renowned for its pristine sandy beaches that cater to various interests. Spend a day sunbathing, picnicking, or building sandcastles at Main Beach, located adjacent to the Santa Cruz

Beach Boardwalk. Visit Seabright State Beach, a popular spot for swimming, volleyball, and beachcombing. Cowell's Beach, with its mellow waves, is perfect for beginners learning to surf. Whether you seek relaxation, water sports, or a lively beach scene, Santa Cruz's beaches have something for everyone.

Santa Cruz Wharf:

Explore the Santa Cruz Wharf, a historic wooden pier that extends into the Monterey Bay. Take a leisurely walk along the pier, enjoy panoramic views of the coastline, and spot sea lions sunbathing on the floating docks. Visit the shops, restaurants, and cafes that line the wharf, offering a taste of local cuisine and souvenirs to commemorate your visit. Don't forget to try the fresh seafood, including clam chowder served in sourdough bread bowls.

Santa Cruz Mountains:

Venture into the nearby Santa Cruz Mountains, a beautiful and lush region that offers a variety of outdoor activities and breathtaking scenery. Explore the redwood forests of Henry Cowell Redwoods State Park, where you can hike among ancient giants andimmerse yourself in the tranquility of nature. Take a scenic drive along Highway 9, winding through picturesque mountain landscapes and charming towns like Boulder Creek and Ben Lomond. Discover hidden waterfalls, such as Berry Creek Falls in Big Basin Redwoods State Park, and enjoy the serenity of the mountain streams and meadows that dot the region.

Pleasure Point:

Experience the laid-back vibes of Pleasure Point, a neighborhood known for its surf breaks and beach town atmosphere. Watch the surfers ride the waves, relax on the sandy shores, or explore the boutiques, cafes, and surf shops that line the streets. Join the locals for a sunset beach bonfire, where you can unwind, roast marshmallows, and enjoy the company of fellow beach lovers.

Santa Cruz Surfing Museum:

Discover the rich history of surfing at the Santa Cruz Surfing Museum, located at Lighthouse Point. Explore the exhibits that showcase the evolution of surfing and its deep-rooted connection to Santa Cruz's coastal culture. Learn about legendary surfers, surfboard designs, and the significant role Santa Cruz has played in the development of the sport. The museum offers a fascinating glimpse into the world of surfing and the vibrant surf community that thrives in Santa Cruz.

Natural History and Wildlife:

Santa Cruz is home to an array of natural wonders and diverse wildlife. Visit the Seymour Marine Discovery Center, where you can learn about the marine ecosystems of Monterey Bay and get up close to marine animals like sharks and sea otters. Explore the University of California Santa Cruz Arboretum and Botanic Garden, which showcases a variety of plant species from around the world. Take a whale-watching tour to witness the migration of gray whales or embark on a bird-watching adventure to spot the numerous bird species that call this area home.

Santa Cruz Downtown:

Discover the vibrant downtown area of Santa Cruz, where you can explore unique shops, art galleries, and local eateries. Stroll along Pacific Avenue, the main thoroughfare, and browse the eclectic mix of boutiques, bookstores, and vintage shops. Visit the Pacific Garden Mall, a pedestrian-friendly outdoor shopping center that hosts street performers and events. Indulge in diverse culinary experiences, from farm-to-table restaurants to international cuisine, and immerse yourself in the lively energy of the city.

Santa Cruz Nightlife:

Experience the vibrant nightlife scene of Santa Cruz, which comes alive with live music, bars, and entertainment venues. Catch a show at the historic Catalyst Club, known for hosting renowned musicians and bands, or enjoy a night of laughter at a comedy club. Dance the night away at local nightclubs or relax with a craft cocktail at one of the many trendy bars in the city. Santa Cruz's nightlife offers a lively and diverse atmosphere for those seeking entertainment after a day of sun and surf.

Santa Cruz invites you to embrace the surf, sun, and beach vibes that define its unique coastal culture. Whether you're a surf enthusiast, a beach lover, or simply seeking a relaxed and laid-back atmosphere, Santa Cruz offers a perfect blend of outdoor adventures, beachfront relaxation, and vibrant coastal charm. Immerse yourself in the surf culture, explore the natural beauty of the region, and create lasting memories in this beach paradise on the Central Coast of California.

Point Reyes National Seashore: Untouched Coastal Wilderness

Welcome to Point Reyes National Seashore, a pristine and untouched coastal wilderness located just north of San Francisco. Situated on the Point Reyes Peninsula, this national seashore offers a unique blend of rugged coastline, scenic landscapes, and abundant wildlife. In this chapter, we will guide you through the essence of Point Reyes National Seashore, showcasing its natural wonders, outdoor activities, and the remarkable experiences that make it a must-visit destination for travelers.

Introduction to Point Reyes National Seashore:

Begin your journey by acquainting yourself with the captivating beauty and ecological significance of Point Reyes National Seashore. This protected area spans over 71,000 acres and encompasses a diverse range of habitats, including coastal bluffs, sandy beaches, estuaries, and forests. Learn about the conservation efforts that have preserved this pristine wilderness and the unique flora and fauna that thrive within its boundaries.

Tomales Point Trail:

Embark on the Tomales Point Trail, a scenic hike that leads to the northernmost tip of the Point Reyes Peninsula. This trail offers breathtaking views of the rugged coastline, rolling hills, and the opportunity to spot tule elk, which are native to the region. As you hike along the narrow peninsula, immerse yourself in the solitude and tranquility of the untouched coastal wilderness.

Chimney Rock:

Visit Chimney Rock, an iconic landmark within Point Reyes National Seashore. This promontory offers stunning views of the Pacific Ocean, the rugged cliffs, and the opportunity to spot migrating gray whales during the winter and spring months. Take a leisurely walk along the trails that wind through wildflowers and coastal grasslands, savoring the panoramic vistas and the refreshing ocean breeze.

Point Reyes Lighthouse:

Explore the historic Point Reyes Lighthouse, perched on the westernmost point of the peninsula. Learn about the rich maritime history of the area and the critical role the lighthouse played in guiding ships along the treacherous coastline. Descend the staircase to the lighthouse, where you can imagine the lives of the keepers who manned this beacon of light. From the observation deck, witness the raw power of the ocean and the dramatic cliffs that surround the lighthouse.

Beaches:

Point Reyes National Seashore is home to several pristine beaches that offer a chance to unwind and connect with nature. Visit Limantour Beach, a wide sandy expanse with dunes and scenic coastal views. Enjoy a picnic or stroll along the shoreline, feeling the soft sand between your toes. Drake's Beach, known for its rugged beauty and stunning sunsets, is a great spot for beachcombing and exploring the tide pools. Whether you seek solitude or a place to enjoy the sun and surf, Point Reyes beaches provide a tranquil escape.

Kayaking and Stand-Up Paddleboarding:

Discover the coastal beauty from a different perspective by embarking on a kayaking or stand-up paddleboarding adventure. Explore Tomales Bay, a narrow inlet that separates the Point Reyes Peninsula from the mainland. Glide through calm waters, marvel at the rocky shoreline, and keep an eye out for harbor seals, sea birds, and other marine life. Whether you're a novice or an experienced paddler, the serenity and natural splendor of Tomales Bay are sure to captivate your senses.

Wildlife Viewing:

Point Reyes National Seashore is a haven for wildlife, offering abundant opportunities for observation and photography. Keep your eyes peeled for the diverse array of bird species that call the seashore home, including snowy egrets, great blue herons, and shorebirds. Spot harbor seals basking on the rocks or catch a glimpse of a majestic tule elk grazing in the grasslands. Join aguided wildlife tour or explore on your own, respecting the animals' natural habitats and maintaining a safe distance.

Tule Elk Reserve:

Venture to the Tule Elk Reserve, a designated area within the national seashore that is home to a population of tule elk, a subspecies native to California. Witness these magnificent creatures in their natural habitat, grazing in grassy meadows or resting in the shade of coastal forests. Learn about the conservation efforts that have helped protect and preserve this iconic species, and gain a deeper appreciation for the delicate balance of nature within the seashore.

Point Reyes Station:

Discover the charming town of Point Reyes Station, located just outside the national seashore. Stroll through the town's quaint streets, lined with art galleries, boutique shops, and farm-to-table restaurants. Sample artisan cheeses, freshly baked goods, and local produce at the town's renowned food establishments. Immerse yourself in the relaxed atmosphere and embrace the community's commitment to sustainability and local craftsmanship.

Point Reyes Shipwreck:

Visit the hauntingly beautiful Point Reyes Shipwreck, also known as the SS Point Reyes. This historic vessel ran aground in 1982 and has since become an iconic landmark on the seashore. The decaying remnants of the ship provide a unique photography opportunity and serve as a reminder of the forces of nature and the power of the ocean.

Point Reyes Bird Observatory:

Explore the Point Reyes Bird Observatory, a renowned research institution dedicated to the study and conservation of birds and their habitats. Learn about ongoing research projects, participate in bird-watching activities, or attend educational programs and workshops. The observatory provides a deeper understanding of the vital role that birds play in the ecosystem and offers a chance to appreciate the diversity and beauty of avian life within Point Reyes National Seashore.

Night Sky Viewing:

Point Reyes National Seashore is a designated International Dark Sky Park, making it an ideal destination for stargazing and night sky photography. On a clear night, the absence of light pollution allows for exceptional views of the stars, planets, and celestial wonders above. Join a guided night sky program or simply find a secluded spot to lay back and marvel at the beauty of the cosmos.

Point Reyes National Seashore invites you to immerse yourself in its untouched coastal wilderness and experience the raw beauty of nature. Whether you're hiking along scenic trails, observing wildlife in their natural habitats, or simply enjoying the tranquility of the beaches, Point Reyes offers a unique opportunity to connect with the land and sea. Embrace the unspoiled beauty, the diverse ecosystems, and the sense of serenity that envelops this coastal gem on the northern California coast.

Sonoma County: Wine, Food, and Outdoor Adventures

Welcome to Sonoma County, a picturesque region in Northern California renowned for its world-class wineries, farm-to-table cuisine, and stunning outdoor landscapes. Nestled between the Pacific Ocean and the Mayacamas Mountains, Sonoma County offers a captivating blend of scenic beauty, cultural richness, and a vibrant culinary scene. In this chapter, we will guide you through the essence of Sonoma County, showcasing its renowned wineries, gastronomic delights, and the remarkable outdoor experiences that make it a must-visit destination for travelers.

Introduction to Sonoma County:

Begin your journey by immersing yourself in the essence of Sonoma County. Discover the region's rich history and heritage as you explore the charming towns, vineyards, and rolling hills that define the area. Learn about the diverse microclimates that contribute to Sonoma's reputation as a premier wine-producing region and understand the significance of sustainable farming practices that have shaped the county's agricultural landscape.

Wine Country:

Sonoma County is synonymous with wine, boasting more than 400 wineries and vineyards. Embark on a wine-tasting adventure through the various wine regions, such as the Russian River Valley, Dry Creek Valley, and Sonoma Valley.

Explore the boutique wineries, family-owned vineyards, and iconic estates, where you can savor award-winning varietals and learn about the winemaking process. Engage with passionate winemakers and discover the unique characteristics that make Sonoma wines distinct.

Farm-to-Table Cuisine:

Indulge in the farm-to-table cuisine that is at the heart of Sonoma County's culinary scene. Visit the local farmers' markets, where you can sample the abundance of fresh, seasonal produce, artisanal cheeses, and locally sourced meats. Dine at acclaimed farm-to-table restaurants, where innovative chefs showcase the flavors of the region in creative and delectable dishes. Immerse yourself in the gastronomic delights and experience the harmonious connection between the land, the farmers, and the chefs.

Sonoma Coast:

Explore the stunning Sonoma Coast, where rugged cliffs, sandy beaches, and picturesque coastal towns await. Take a leisurely drive along Highway 1, reveling in the panoramic views of the Pacific Ocean and the rugged beauty of the coastline. Discover hidden coves, such as Bodega Bay and Jenner, where you can beachcomb, go tidepooling, or simply enjoy a scenic picnic while listening to the crashing waves. The Sonoma Coast offers a serene and awe-inspiring escape from the bustle of everyday life.

Redwood Forests:

Venture into the majestic redwood forests of Sonoma County, where ancient giants stand tall in tranquil groves. Visit Armstrong Redwoods State Natural Reserve, home to some of the tallest and oldest trees in the region. Take a peaceful hike through the towering redwoods, allowing their presence to inspire and rejuvenate your spirit. Connect with nature, breathe in the fresh forest air, and embrace the tranquility of these awe-inspiring natural wonders.

Outdoor Adventures:

Sonoma County is a playground for outdoor enthusiasts, offering a plethora of activities for all ages and interests. Explore the diverse landscapes through hiking, mountain biking, or horseback riding along the extensive network of trails that wind through the county. Kayak or paddleboard along the Russian River, meandering through vineyard-dotted valleys and picturesque countryside. Embark on a hot air balloon ride, soaring above the vineyards and taking in panoramic views of the rolling hills. Sonoma County's natural beauty invites you to embark on unforgettable outdoor adventures.

Sonoma Plaza:

Visit Sonoma Plaza, the heart of the historic town of Sonoma. This charming and picturesque plaza issurrounded by boutiques, tasting rooms, and restaurants, offering a delightful blend of history, culture, and culinary delights. Explore the adobe buildings that date back to the Spanish colonial era, visit the Sonoma State Historic Park, or simply relax in the park's shaded lawns while enjoying a picnic. Sonoma Plaza is a vibrant hub where locals and visitors come together to celebrate the region's rich heritage and vibrant community spirit.

Sonoma Valley:

Delve into the idyllic beauty of Sonoma Valley, known as the birthplace of California's wine industry. Meander through scenic vineyards, where you can witness the winemaking process firsthand, participate in grape harvests, or even try your hand at blending your own wine. Discover the charming town of Glen Ellen, once home to renowned writer Jack London, and explore his historic estate, now a state historic park. Sonoma Valley offers a quintessential wine country experience, with its rolling hills, charming estates, and unparalleled wine tastings.

Hot Springs and Wellness Retreats:

Unwind and rejuvenate at the hot springs and wellness retreats scattered throughout Sonoma County. Immerse yourself in healing mineral waters that have drawn visitors seeking relaxation and rejuvenation for centuries. Indulge in spa treatments, soak in natural hot springs, or embark on a wellness retreat that nourishes your mind, body, and soul. Let the healing powers of Sonoma County's hot springs restore balance and serenity to your life.

Art and Culture:

Sonoma County is a vibrant hub of artistic expression and cultural diversity. Explore the numerous art galleries, studios, and performance venues that showcase the talents of local artists and performers. Attend live music concerts, theater productions, or art festivals that celebrate the creative spirit of the region. Immerse yourself in the artistic energy that permeates Sonoma County and discover the unique cultural tapestry that thrives within its borders.

Sonoma County Parks:

Discover the natural beauty and recreational opportunities offered by Sonoma County's parks. From the sprawling Hood Mountain Regional Park to the scenic Spring Lake Regional Park, these natural oases provide opportunities for hiking, picnicking, fishing, and wildlife observation. Engage in birdwatching at Shollenberger Park or explore the rugged terrain of Annadel State Park. Sonoma County's parks offer a chance to connect with nature, recharge your spirit, and create lasting memories in the great outdoors.

Sustainability and Organic Farming:

Sonoma County embraces sustainable and organic farming practices, making it a leader in the farm-to-table movement. Engage with local farmers, vintners, and producers who prioritize environmentally friendly and socially responsible practices. Visit organic farms and vineyards that showcase the harmony between agriculture and conservation. Learn about the region's commitment to sustainable viticulture, organic produce, and the preservation of the natural beauty that defines Sonoma County.

Sonoma County invites you to embark on a sensory journey of wine, food, and outdoor adventures. Indulge in the flavors of the region, explore the stunning landscapes, and immerse yourself in the warmth of the local communities. From savoring award-winning wines to hiking among ancient redwoods, Sonoma County offers a captivating experience that nourishes both body and soul. Embrace the abundant natural beauty, the richness of the culinary scene, and the warm hospitality that awaits you in this enchanting destination.

Humboldt County: Where Nature and Culture Meet

Welcome to Humboldt County, a captivating region in Northern California where the beauty of nature merges seamlessly with a rich cultural tapestry. Nestled along the Pacific coast, Humboldt County is renowned for its towering redwood forests, pristine coastline, and vibrant arts scene. In this chapter, we will guide you through the essence of Humboldt County, showcasing its natural wonders, cultural heritage, and the remarkable experiences that make it a must-visit destination for travelers.

Introduction to Humboldt County:

Begin your journey by immersing yourself in the essence of Humboldt County. Discover the region's unique blend of natural beauty and cultural diversity as you explore the ancient redwood forests, scenic coastal landscapes, and charming towns. Learn about the indigenous peoples who have inhabited this land for thousands of years and the vibrant communities that call Humboldt County home.

Avenue of the Giants:

Embark on a mesmerizing drive along the Avenue of the Giants, a scenic stretch of Highway 101 that winds through Humboldt County's majestic redwood forests. Marvel at the towering giants that line the road, creating a cathedral-like atmosphere of tranquility and awe. Take a leisurely hike through the ancient groves, where shafts of sunlight filter through the dense canopy, illuminating the moss-covered forest floor. The Avenue of the Giants offers a humbling and unforgettable experience in the presence of these majestic natural wonders.

Redwood National and State Parks:

Explore the renowned Redwood National and State Parks, a UNESCO World Heritage site and home to the tallest trees on Earth. Hike through the diverse ecosystems of the parks, from old-growth forests to fern-filled canyons. Stand in awe beneath the towering giants, their immense size and age providing a profound connection to the natural world. Experience the tranquility of the parks' pristine rivers, coastal dunes, and wildlife-rich estuaries. The Redwood National and State Parks offer a sanctuary of breathtaking beauty and a reminder of the importance of conservation.

Coastal Splendor:

Discover the rugged coastal beauty of Humboldt County, where dramatic cliffs, rocky shorelines, and pristine beaches await. Explore Trinidad, a picturesque seaside town known for its scenic vistas, historic lighthouse, and vibrant art scene. Hike along the Trinidad Head Trail, where you can witness panoramic views of the Pacific Ocean and spot migrating whales during the winter months. Visit Patrick's Point State Park, where you can explore tide pools, hike through old-growth forests, and witness breathtaking sunsets over the rugged coastline.

Avenue of the Arts:

Immerse yourself in the vibrant arts scene of Humboldt County by exploring the Avenue of the Arts in Eureka. Discover galleries, studios, and boutiques that showcase the work of local artists, from paintings and sculptures to jewelry and textiles. Visit the Morris Graves Museum of Art, which features a diverse collection of contemporary and traditional works, as well as rotating exhibitions that highlight the talent and creativity of Humboldt County's artistic community. The Avenue of the Arts offers a vibrant and eclectic blend of artistic expression.

Ferndale:

Step back in time as you visit the historic Victorian village of Ferndale. Stroll through the well-preserved downtown area, where impeccably restored 19th-century buildings house charming shops, art galleries, and eateries. Admire the ornate Victorian architecture, take a horse-drawn carriage ride through the streets, or simply soak in the small-town charm that permeates Ferndale. This quaint town offers a glimpse into the region's rich history and architectural heritage.

Humboldt Bay:

Explore the natural and cultural treasures of Humboldt Bay, the largest enclosed bay on the California coast. Take a scenic boat tour or kayakalong the bay's intricate network of waterways, where you can spot a variety of bird species, including herons, egrets, and migratory waterfowl. Visit the Humboldt Bay National Wildlife Refuge, which provides habitat for a diverse range of wildlife and offers opportunities for birdwatching, hiking, and photography. Learn about the bay's maritime history at the Humboldt Bay Maritime Museum, where exhibits showcase the region's connection to the sea and its rich maritime heritage.

Avenue of the Giants Marathon:

Participate in the Avenue of the Giants Marathon, an annual event that attracts runners from around the world. Experience the thrill of running amidst the towering redwoods, with the scent of ancient forest and the cheers of spectators propelling you forward. Whether you're a seasoned marathoner or a recreational runner, the Avenue of the Giants Marathon offers a unique and unforgettable racing experience.

Humboldt State University and Arcata:

Visit Humboldt State University, located in the vibrant town of Arcata. Explore the campus, known for its beautiful redwood setting, and discover the university's commitment to environmental sustainability and social justice. Enjoy the lively atmosphere of Arcata, with its colorful Victorian buildings, local shops, and lively farmers' markct. Engagc with the intellectual and cultural vitality of the university community, attend a performance at the Van Duzer Theatre, or explore the natural beauty of the surrounding areas.

Trinidad Head Light:

Visit the Trinidad Head Light, a historic lighthouse perched atop Trinidad Head. Take a short hike to the lighthouse, where you can learn about its history and enjoy panoramic views of the rugged coastline. Explore the interpretive panels that provide insight into the area's maritime heritage and the role of the lighthouse in guiding ships to safety. The Trinidad Head Light offers a glimpse into the region's rich maritime history and a vantage point to appreciate the beauty of the Pacific Ocean.

Local Cuisine and Farmers' Markets:

Savor the flavors of Humboldt County by indulging in its diverse culinary offerings. Enjoy farm-to-table dining experiences that highlight the region's abundance of fresh produce, artisanal cheeses, and locally sourced ingredients. Visit the farmers' markets in Arcata and Eureka, where you can taste the bounty of the land and connect with local farmers, bakers, and artisans. Immerse yourself in the vibrant culinary scene and discover the unique flavors that define Humboldt County.

Outdoor Recreation:

Humboldt County offers a plethora of outdoor recreational opportunities for nature enthusiasts. Hike through the expansive network of trails in the Six Rivers National Forest, where you can explore dense forests, sparkling rivers, and cascading waterfalls. Kayak or paddleboard along the Eel River, the Mattole River, or the Humboldt Bay, immersing yourself in the tranquility of these pristine waterways. Engage in fishing, birdwatching, or camping in the region's numerous parks and wilderness areas. Humboldt County's natural beauty invites you to embrace the spirit of adventure and connect with the wilderness.

Humboldt County welcomes you with open arms, inviting you to explore its breathtaking landscapes, immerse yourself in its vibrant arts scene, and embrace its rich cultural heritage. From the towering redwoods to the rugged coastline, from the lively towns to the serene wilderness, Humboldt County offers a harmonious blend of nature and culture that will leave you with lasting memories and a deep appreciation for this captivating corner of Northern California.

Exploring Lassen Volcanic National Park

Welcome to Lassen Volcanic National Park, a geological wonderland nestled in the rugged landscapes of Northern California. Known for its volcanic peaks, hydrothermal features, and pristine wilderness, Lassen Volcanic National Park offers visitors a unique opportunity to witness the forces of nature at work. In this chapter, we will guide you through the essence of Lassen Volcanic National Park, showcasing its diverse landscapes, fascinating geology, and the remarkable experiences that make it a must-visit destination for travelers.

Introduction to Lassen Volcanic National Park:

Begin your journey by immersing yourself in the geological and natural wonders that define Lassen Volcanic National Park. Learn about the park's volcanic history, which includes the eruptions of Mount Lassen in the early 20th century, and understand the significance of the area's hydrothermal features. Discover the unique blend of natural beauty, outdoor recreation, and scientific significance that makes Lassen Volcanic National Park a captivating destination.

Lassen Peak:

Embark on an unforgettable hike to the summit of Lassen Peak, the park's most iconic volcano. Ascend through alpine meadows and scree fields as you make your way to the top, where panoramic views of the surrounding landscapes await. Marvel at the sight of the devastated landscape caused by the volcano's eruptions, and gain a deeper appreciation for the power of nature. The hike to Lassen Peak is a challenging yet rewarding experience that offers a glimpse into the volcanic history of the region.

Bumpass Hell:

Visit Bumpass Hell, the park's largest and most famous hydrothermal area. Explore a boardwalk trail that leads you through a landscape of boiling mud pots, steaming fumaroles, and colorful hot springs. Witness the raw power of geothermal activity as steam rises from the earth, and the pungent smell of sulfur fills the air. Learn about the geology and the unique microbial life that thrives in these extreme conditions. Bumpass Hell provides a mesmerizing and otherworldly experience that showcases the dynamic nature of Lassen Volcanic National Park.

Lake Helen and Reflection Lake:

Discover the serene beauty of Lake Helen and Reflection Lake, two picturesque alpine lakes located within the park. Take a leisurely hike around their shores, admire the crystal-clear waters, and capture stunning reflections of the surrounding volcanic peaks. These tranquil lakes offer a peaceful retreat and a chance to connect with the pristine wilderness that characterizes Lassen Volcanic National Park.

Cinder Cone:

Venture to Cinder Cone, a volcanic cone

formed by the eruption of the Fantastic Lava Beds thousands of years ago. Embark on a challenging hike to the summit, where you will be rewarded with panoramic views of the surrounding landscapes, including the Painted Dunes, an area characterized by colorful volcanic ash deposits. Descend into the crater of Cinder Cone, where you can explore the eerie landscape and imagine the powerful volcanic forces that shaped the area.

Summit Lake:

Enjoy the beauty and tranquility of Summit Lake, a peaceful alpine lake nestled among volcanic landscapes. Take a leisurely stroll along the lakeshore, picnic amidst wildflowers, or embark on a kayak or paddleboard adventure on its pristine waters. Summit Lake provides a scenic oasis where you can relax and immerse yourself in the natural splendor of Lassen Volcanic National Park.

Hiking and Backcountry Exploration:

Lassen Volcanic National Park offers an extensive network of hiking trails that cater to all levels of experience. From easy nature walks to challenging backcountry treks, there are options for every adventurer. Explore the park's diverse landscapes, including meadows, forests, and volcanic peaks. Backpackthrough the remote wilderness and camp under the starlit skies, connecting with nature in its purest form. Immerse yourself in the serenity and solitude of the backcountry, where you can discover hidden lakes, cascading waterfalls, and untouched landscapes.

Sulphur Works:

Experience the geothermal wonders of Sulphur Works, a hydrothermal area accessible by a short hike or a scenic drive. Witness the bubbling mud pots and steaming vents as you learn about the park's volcanic activity and the geological processes that create these unique features. Enjoy the therapeutic effects of the natural hot springs that flow through Sulphur Works, known for their mineral-rich waters. Relax and rejuvenate in this surreal landscape of steam and vibrant colors.

Devastated Area:

Explore the Devastated Area, a landscape still recovering from the eruptions of Mount Lassen in the early 20th century. Take a self-guided tour along the accessible Devastated Area Interpretive Trail, where interpretive signs provide insight into the volcanic eruptions and the subsequent ecological recovery. Witness the stark contrast between the barren volcanic landscape and the gradual return of plant and animal life. The Devastated Area offers a poignant reminder of the forces of nature and the resilience of the natural world.

Wildlife Viewing:

Lassen Volcanic National Park is home to a diverse array of wildlife, including black bears, mule deer, mountain lions, and a variety of bird species. Keep your eyes peeled for these magnificent creatures as you explore the park's trails and meadows. Birdwatchers will delight in the opportunity to spot species such as the white-headed woodpecker and the western tanager. Wildlife viewing in Lassen Volcanic National Park provides a chance to connect with the natural inhabitants of this pristine wilderness.

Ranger Programs and Interpretive Centers:

Engage with the park's knowledgeable rangers and participate in interpretive programs that delve deeper into the geology, ecology, and cultural history of Lassen Volcanic National Park. Attend guided hikes, campfire talks, or stargazing programs to enhance your understanding and appreciation of the park's natural wonders. Visit the park's visitor centers, including the Kohm Yah-mah-nee Visitor Center and the Loomis Museum, where exhibits and displays offer a glimpse into the park's geological features, natural history, and cultural significance.

Winter Adventures:

Embrace the winter wonderland of Lassen Volcanic National Park, where snow-covered landscapes provide a playground for winter sports enthusiasts. Enjoy cross-country skiing or snowshoeing along the park's trails, immersing yourself in the tranquility of the winter forest. Join a ranger-led snowshoe walk to learn about the park's winter ecology and witness the beauty of the snow-covered volcanic peaks. Lassen Volcanic National Park transforms into a magical winter landscape, offering unique experiences for those who venture into its snowy realms.

Lassen Volcanic National Park invites you to explore its remarkable landscapes, witness its volcanic activity, and immerse yourself in its pristine wilderness. Whether you're hiking to the summit of a volcano, soaking in a natural hot spring, or marveling at the colorful hydrothermal features, Lassen Volcanic National Park promises an awe-inspiring journey through the dynamic forces of nature. Embrace the geological wonders, embrace the diversity of the park's ecosystems, and create lasting memories in this captivating corner of Northern California.

Shasta Cascade: Lakes, Mountains, and Outdoor Bliss

Welcome to the Shasta Cascade region, a breathtaking corner of Northern California where lakes, mountains, and pristine wilderness beckon outdoor enthusiasts. From the majestic Mount Shasta to the sparkling lakes and cascading waterfalls, the Shasta Cascade offers a wealth of natural wonders and exhilarating adventures. In this chapter, we will guide you through the essence of the Shasta Cascade, showcasing its stunning landscapes, outdoor activities, and the remarkable experiences that make it a must-visit destination for travelers.

Introduction to the Shasta Cascade:

Begin your journey by immersing yourself in the natural splendor and outdoor bliss that define the Shasta Cascade region. Learn about the region's geological features, including the towering volcanic peak of Mount Shasta and the cascading waterways that flow through the area. Discover the diverse ecosystems that make the Shasta Cascade a haven for wildlife and outdoor enthusiasts alike.

Mount Shasta:

Embrace the awe-inspiring presence of Mount Shasta, one of the highest peaks in the Cascade Range. Hike through alpine meadows and old-growth forests as you make your way to the summit, where breathtaking panoramic views await. Mount Shasta offers a range of hiking options, from day hikes to multi-day expeditions, catering to all levels of experience. Immerse yourself in the serene beauty of this majestic mountain and let its towering presence inspire a sense of wonder and adventure.

Shasta Lake:

Discover the shimmering jewel of the Shasta Cascade, Shasta Lake. This expansive reservoir offers endless opportunities for water-based recreation, including boating, fishing, swimming, and paddleboarding. Explore the secluded coves and hidden beaches, where you can relax and soak up the sun. Shasta Lake is also a popular destination for houseboating, allowing you to immerse yourself in the beauty of the lake and its surrounding landscapes.

Burney Falls:

Marvel at the spectacular Burney Falls, often referred to as the "Eighth Wonder of the World." This 129-foot waterfall, located within McArthur-Burney Falls Memorial State Park, cascades down a moss-covered cliff, creating a mesmerizing display of nature's power and beauty. Take a hike along the park's trails, where you can witness the falls from various viewpoints and appreciate the serenity of the surrounding forest. Burney Falls is a true natural gem that captivates visitors with its timeless beauty.

Lassen Volcanic National Park:

Explore the captivating landscapes of Lassen Volcanic National Park, where volcanic peaks, hydrothermal features, and pristine wilderness await. Hike through scenic trails that wind through sulfur-scented fumaroles, bubbling mud pots, and colorful hot springs. Witness the volcanic activity at Bumpass Hell or embark on a challenging hike to the summit of Lassen Peak. Lassen Volcanic National Park offers a unique blend of geological wonders and outdoor adventures that will leave you in awe.

Trinity Alps Wilderness:

Venture into the remote and rugged wilderness of the Trinity Alps, a mountain range renowned for its breathtaking beauty and exceptional hiking opportunities. Embark on multi-day backpacking trips through alpine meadows, traverse granite peaks, and swim in pristine mountain lakes. Explore the myriad of trails that wind through the Trinity Alps Wilderness, where solitude and natural beauty await at every turn. This untouched wilderness provides a true escape into the heart of nature.

Whiskeytown National Recreation Area:

Immerse yourself in the recreational opportunities offered by Whiskeytown National Recreation Area, located west of Redding. Discover crystal-clear lakes, scenic waterfalls, and verdant forests as you kayak, paddleboard, or swim in the refreshing waters of Whiskeytown Lake. Explorethe park's numerous hiking trails, where you can encounter hidden waterfalls, spot wildlife, and immerse yourself in the serenity of nature. Visit the historic Whiskeytown Falls, a 220-foot waterfall that cascades through lush vegetation, offering a tranquil and picturesque setting. Whiskeytown National Recreation Area invites you to indulge in outdoor adventures and create lasting memories in its natural playground.

Castle Crags State Park:

Marvel at the dramatic granite spires of Castle Crags State Park, located south of Mount Shasta. Hike along the park's trails, which offer stunning views of the towering crags and the surrounding landscapes. Explore the Castle Dome Trail, a challenging hike that rewards you with panoramic vistas of the rugged wilderness. Castle Crags State Park is a paradise for rock climbers, with its granite cliffs providing thrilling climbing opportunities for both novice and experienced climbers.

Lake Almanor:

Discover the beauty of Lake Almanor, a serene mountain lake surrounded by lush forests and breathtaking vistas. Enjoy a variety of water activities, including boating, fishing, and swimming, or simply relax on the sandy shores and soak in the tranquility of the surroundings. Lake Almanor is a popular destination for anglers, with its abundant populations of trout, bass, and salmon. Embrace the peaceful ambiance and natural splendor of this hidden gem in the Shasta Cascade.

Ahjumawi Lava Springs State Park:

Experience the unique landscapes of

Ahjumawi Lava Springs State Park, located east of Mount Shasta. Explore a network of waterways and paddle through a series of scenic lakes, marshes, and lava tube caves. Witness the remnants of volcanic activity as you navigate through the park's fascinating geology. Ahjumawi Lava Springs State Park offers a peaceful retreat and a chance to connect with nature in its raw and untouched form.

Pacific Crest Trail:

Trace a portion of the iconic Pacific Crest Trail as it winds through the Shasta Cascade region. Embark on a day hike or a multi-day backpacking adventure, immersing yourself in the stunning landscapes and solitude of the trail. Experience the thrill of hiking through diverse ecosystems, crossing mountain passes, and encountering fellow hikers along the way. The Pacific Crest Trail offers an unforgettable journey through the natural wonders of the Shasta Cascade.

Outdoor Recreation and Wildlife Viewing:

The Shasta Cascade region provides endless opportunities for outdoor recreation and wildlife viewing. Engage in activities such as mountain biking, rock climbing, birdwatching, and wildlife photography. Observe elusive wildlife species, including black bears, bald eagles, and ospreys, as you explore the diverse landscapes. The region's abundant natural beauty invites you to embrace the spirit of adventure, connect with the wilderness, and create unforgettable memories.

The Shasta Cascade region offers a haven for outdoor enthusiasts, where lakes, mountains, and pristine wilderness await exploration. Whether you're hiking through ancient forests, kayaking on sparkling lakes, or marveling at towering waterfalls, the Shasta Cascade promises exhilarating adventures and a profound connection with nature. Embrace the natural wonders, embrace the spirit of outdoor bliss, and immerse yourself in the breathtaking landscapes of this remarkable corner of Northern California.

Exploring the San Francisco Bay Area

Welcome to the vibrant and diverse San Francisco Bay Area, a cultural and technological hub that combines stunning natural beauty with a bustling urban atmosphere. From the iconic Golden Gate Bridge to the rolling vineyards of Napa Valley, the San Francisco Bay Area offers a multitude of experiences for every traveler. In this chapter, we will guide you through the essence of the Bay Area, showcasing its iconic landmarks, diverse neighborhoods, and the remarkable experiences that make it a must-visit destination for travelers.

Introduction to the San Francisco Bay Area:

Begin your journey by immersing yourself in the essence of the San Francisco Bay Area. Learn about the region's rich history, from the Spanish colonization to the California Gold Rush, and understand its cultural and economic significance. Discover the unique blend of diverse communities, cutting-edge technology, and natural beauty that make the Bay Area a captivating destination.

San Francisco:

Explore the vibrant city of San Francisco, known for its steep hills, eclectic neighborhoods, and iconic landmarks. Take a stroll along the historic waterfront of Fisherman's Wharf, where you can savor fresh seafood, visit the famous sea lions at Pier 39, or embark on a boat tour to Alcatraz Island. Explore the colorful streets of Chinatown, the largest Chinatown outside of Asia, where you can sample authentic cuisine and browse unique shops. Don't miss the opportunity to walk or bike across the majestic Golden Gate Bridge, one of the world's most famous suspension bridges. San Francisco offers a multitude of experiences, from exploring its world-class museums to enjoying panoramic views from its famous hills.

Marin County:

Cross the Golden Gate Bridge and venture into Marin County, a picturesque region known for its stunning coastal landscapes and idyllic towns. Visit the charming town of Sausalito, where you can stroll along the waterfront, explore art galleries, and enjoy waterfront dining with views of the San Francisco skyline. Discover the natural beauty of Marin County by hiking through the Marin Headlands or exploring the Point Reyes National Seashore, where you can spot wildlife, visit historic lighthouses, and enjoy scenic coastal vistas.

Silicon Valley:

Explore the epicenter of technology and innovation in Silicon Valley, home to some of the world's most influential tech companies. Visit the campuses of tech giants such as Google, Apple, and Facebook, where you can learn about their cutting-edge innovations and the impact they have on our daily lives. Immerse yourself in the entrepreneurial spirit of the region by visiting startup incubators, attending tech conferences, or exploring interactive museums that showcase the latest advancements in technology.

Berkeley and the East Bay:

Experience the vibrant energy of Berkeley and the East Bay, known for its thriving arts scene, cultural diversity, and renowned universities. Visit the University of California, Berkeley campus, where you can explore its beautiful grounds, visit museums, and attend lectures or performances. Stroll along the lively Telegraph Avenue, lined with unique shops, cafes, and street performers. Discover the culinary delights of the Gourmet Ghetto, home to world-class restaurants and food artisans. The East Bay offers a dynamic blend of intellectualism, cultural expression, and culinary excellence.

Napa Valley and Sonoma County:

Indulge in the world-famous wines and scenic beauty of Napa Valley and Sonoma County. Take a leisurely drive through rolling vineyards, stopping at renowned wineries for tastings and tours. Visit charming towns such as Yountville, St. Helena, and Healdsburg, where you can savor farm-to-table cuisine, browse art galleries, and relax in luxurious spas. Immerse yourself in the winemaking process by participating in grape harvests or blending your own wine. Napa Valley and Sonoma County offer a trueescape into the world of wine, where you can savor the flavors, embrace the beauty of the vineyards, and experience the warm hospitality of the region.

Oakland:

Discover the vibrant and culturally diverse city of Oakland, located on the eastern side of the San Francisco Bay. Explore the bustling neighborhoods of downtown Oakland, Jack London Square, and the Uptown district, where you can find an array of art galleries, live music venues, and gourmet restaurants. Visit the Oakland Museum of California, which showcases the state's rich history, art, and culture. Explore the beautiful Lake Merritt, a urban oasis where you can walk, bike, or enjoy a boat ride. Oakland offers a vibrant blend of art, culture, and a thriving culinary scene.

Peninsula and South Bay:

Experience the beauty and innovation of the Peninsula and South Bay, home to iconic landmarks and technological advancements. Explore the Stanford University campus, renowned for its academic excellence and stunning architecture. Visit the Computer History Museum in Mountain View, where you can learn about the evolution of computing and the impact of Silicon Valley. Discover the natural beauty of the Peninsula by hiking through the Santa Cruz Mountains or exploring the coastal towns of Half Moon Bay and Pacifica. The Peninsula and South Bay offer a harmonious blend of natural beauty and technological achievements.

Santa Cruz:

Embrace the laid-back beach vibes of Santa Cruz, a coastal town known for its surf culture, scenic beaches, and the Santa Cruz Beach Boardwalk. Relax on the sandy shores, catch a wave at renowned surf spots, or stroll along the iconic Santa Cruz Wharf. Explore the Santa Cruz Mountains, where you can hike through towering redwoods or visit wineries that specialize in cool-climate varietals. Santa Cruz embodies the quintessential California beach town, offering a perfect blend of outdoor adventure and beachside relaxation.

Redwood City and the Mid-Peninsula:

Discover the charm and natural beauty of Redwood City and the Mid-Peninsula region. Explore the hidden gem of Filoli Historic House and Gardens, a magnificent estate with stunning gardens and a historic mansion. Immerse yourself in the serenity of the nearby Redwood City saltwater marshes, where you can observe a variety of bird species and enjoy peaceful nature walks. Discover the vibrant downtown areas of Redwood City and nearby Palo Alto, where you can find a mix of independent shops, restaurants, and cultural attractions. The Mid-Peninsula region offers a tranquil escape and a chance to connect with nature and local communities.

San Jose:

Experience the dynamic city of San Jose, the largest city in the Bay Area and the cultural hub of Silicon Valley. Visit the Tech Museum of Innovation, where you can engage with interactive exhibits that showcase the latest advancements in science and technology. Explore the vibrant downtown area, known as San Pedro Square, where you can find a variety of restaurants, bars, and live music venues. Discover the rich cultural heritage of San Jose by visiting the San Jose Museum of Art, the Mexican Heritage Plaza, or the historic Japantown neighborhood. San Jose offers a perfect blend of technology, arts, and cultural diversity.

Outdoor Recreation and Natural Beauty:

The San Francisco Bay Area is renowned for its natural beauty and outdoor recreational opportunities. Whether you want to hike in the Marin Headlands, bike across the Golden Gate Bridge, or explore the Point Reyes National Seashore, there are endless options for outdoor adventures. Enjoy a scenic drive along Highway 1, where you can witness breathtaking coastal vistas and rugged landscapes. The Bay Area offers a multitude of parks, trails, and beaches that invite you to embrace the beauty of nature and create unforgettable memories.

The San Francisco Bay Area invites you to explore its diverse neighborhoods, embrace its cultural richness, and immerse yourself inthe natural and technological wonders that define this captivating region. From the iconic landmarks of San Francisco to the vineyards of Napa Valley, from the cultural vibrancy of Oakland to the innovation of Silicon Valley, the Bay Area offers a blend of experiences that cater to every traveler's interests. Embrace the charm, embrace the diversity, and embark on a journey of exploration in this dynamic and captivating corner of Northern California.

Wine Tasting in Northern California: A Complete Guide

Welcome to the wine paradise of Northern California, where rolling vineyards, picturesque wineries, and world-class wines await. From the renowned Napa Valley to the charming winemaking regions of Sonoma County and beyond, Northern California offers a wine tasting experience like no other. In this chapter, we will guide you through the essence of wine tasting in Northern California, showcasing the diverse wine regions, notable wineries, and the remarkable experiences that make it a must-visit destination for wine enthusiasts.

Introduction to Wine Tasting in Northern California:

Begin your journey by immersing yourself in the rich wine heritage and winemaking traditions of Northern California. Learn about the unique characteristics of the region's wine regions, including the Mediterranean climate, diverse soil types, and the influence of cooling coastal breezes. Discover the world-class wines produced in Northern California and understand the dedication and craftsmanship that goes into each bottle.

Napa Valley:

Explore the crown jewel of Northern California's wine regions, Napa Valley. With its prestigious wineries, scenic landscapes, and luxurious accommodations, Napa Valley is a wine lover's dream come true. Visit renowned wineries such as Robert Mondavi, Opus One, and Stag's Leap Wine Cellars, where you can savor award-winning wines and immerse yourself in the art of winemaking. Take a leisurely drive along the Silverado Trail or the iconic Highway 29, where vineyards stretch as far as the eye can see. Indulge in farm-to-table cuisine at Michelin-starred restaurants and experience the ultimate in wine and culinary pairings. Napa Valley offers a sophisticated and unforgettable wine tasting experience.

Sonoma County:

Discover the laid-back charm and diverse wine offerings of Sonoma County. With its distinct microclimates and varied terroir, Sonoma County produces a wide range of wines, from Chardonnay and Pinot Noir to Zinfandel and Cabernet Sauvignon. Explore the Russian River Valley, known for its cool-climate wines and stunning vineyard vistas. Visit the quaint town of Healdsburg, where you can find boutique wineries and enjoy a relaxed wine tasting experience. Explore the Sonoma Valley, where historic wineries and family-owned vineyards offer a glimpse into the region's winemaking heritage. Sonoma County invites you to savor its diverse wine varietals and embrace its welcoming and unpretentious atmosphere.

Mendocino County:

Venture north to Mendocino County, a hidden gem of Northern California's wine regions. Known for its rugged coastline, towering redwoods, and boutique wineries, Mendocino County offers a unique wine tasting experience in a stunning natural setting. Explore the Anderson Valley, famous for its cool-climate wines such as Pinot Noir and Alsatian varietals. Visit the quaint town of Ukiah and its surrounding vineyards, where you can taste organic and biodynamic wines crafted with sustainable practices. Mendocino County is a wine destination off the beaten path, where you can discover hidden gems and enjoy a more intimate and personal wine tasting experience.

Sierra Foothills:

Embrace the charm and rustic beauty of the Sierra Foothills, a lesser-known but thriving wine region in Northern California. With its higher elevation and diverse microclimates, the Sierra Foothills is known for its bold red wines, including Zinfandel, Syrah, and Barbera. Explore the historic Gold Rush towns of Placerville and Nevada City, where boutique wineries offer unique wine varietals and a laid-back atmosphere. The Sierra Foothills is a wine region with a rich history and a commitment to producing exceptional wines that reflect the region's distinctterroir.

Livermore Valley:

Discover the wine heritage of the Livermore Valley, one of California's oldest wine regions. Located east of San Francisco, the Livermore Valley is known for its Mediterranean climate and diverse wine offerings. Explore wineries such as

Wente Vineyards and Concannon Vineyard, which have played a significant role in shaping California's wine industry. Visit the historic downtown area of Livermore, where you can find wine bars, restaurants, and charming shops. The Livermore Valley offers a blend of tradition and innovation, making it a captivating wine tasting destination.

Santa Cruz Mountains:

Indulge in the cool-climate wines and breathtaking vistas of the Santa Cruz Mountains. Nestled between the Pacific Ocean and the Silicon Valley, the Santa Cruz Mountains wine region offers a unique combination of coastal influences and mountain terroir. Visit wineries such as Ridge Vineyards and Mount Eden Vineyards, where you can taste exceptional Chardonnay, Pinot Noir, and Cabernet Sauvignon. Enjoy panoramic views of the vineyards and the surrounding landscapes as you sip on world-class wines. The Santa Cruz Mountains provide a serene and picturesque wine tasting experience.

Amador County:

Experience the old-world charm and rich winemaking history of Amador County. Located in the Sierra Nevada foothills, Amador County is known for its robust Zinfandels and other Mediterranean varietals. Explore the quaint towns of Plymouth and Sutter Creek, where you can find family-owned wineries and tasting rooms. Enjoy the scenic beauty of the region as you sample wines that reflect the area's unique terroir and winemaking traditions. Amador County offers a warm and welcoming wine tasting experience.

Paso Robles:

Venture south to Paso Robles, a burgeoning wine region that has gained recognition for its bold red wines and innovative winemakers. With its warm days and cool nights, Paso Robles is ideal for growing Rhône and Bordeaux varietals. Visit wineries such as Tablas Creek Vineyard and Justin Vineyards & Winery, where you can taste exceptional wines and experience the region's commitment to sustainable and organic practices. Paso Robles offers a relaxed and down-to-earth wine tasting experience, with a focus on quality and craftsmanship.

Wine Tours and Experiences:

Make the most of your wine tasting journey in Northern California by joining wine tours and immersive experiences. Hop on a guided wine tour that takes you through the scenic vineyards, offering insight into the winemaking process and the region's unique characteristics. Participate in vineyard hikes, blending seminars, or wine pairing dinners that provide a deeper understanding and appreciation for the wines of Northern California. Engage with winemakers, sommeliers, and wine enthusiasts who share their expertise and passion. Wine tours and experiences add an extra layer of enjoyment and education to your wine tasting adventure.

Wine and Culinary Delights:

Pair your wine tasting experiences with the culinary delights of Northern California. Many wineries offer food and wine pairing experiences, where you can savor local artisanal cheeses, charcuterie, and gourmet dishes that complement the wines perfectly. Explore the farm-to-table cuisine of the region, which emphasizes fresh, local ingredients that enhance the wine tasting experience. Northern California's vibrant food scene provides a perfect accompaniment to the world-class wines produced in the region.

Wine Country Hospitality:

Northern California's wine regions are known for their warm hospitality and welcoming atmosphere. Whether you're visiting a small family-owned winery or a grand estate, you'll find passionate winemakers and knowledgeable staff who are eager to share their love for wine. Engage in conversations about winemaking techniques, vineyard management, and the unique characteristics of each wine. Thepeople of Northern California's wine country embody a genuine and friendly spirit that enhances the wine tasting experience.

Wine tasting in Northern California is a journey of exploration and appreciation. From the world-renowned vineyards of Napa Valley to the hidden gems of Mendocino County, each wine region offers a distinct and unforgettable experience. Embrace the beauty of the vineyards, savor the flavors of exceptional wines, and immerse yourself in the rich winemaking heritage of Northern California. Cheers to a wine tasting adventure filled with discovery, enjoyment, and the creation of lasting memories.

Outdoor Adventures in Northern California

Welcome to the outdoor enthusiast's paradise of Northern California, where breathtaking landscapes, diverse ecosystems, and exhilarating adventures await. From the towering redwoods to the rugged coastline, and from the majestic mountains to the pristine lakes and rivers, Northern California offers a plethora of outdoor activities for every adventurer. In this chapter, we will guide you through the essence of outdoor adventures in Northern California, showcasing the region's iconic natural wonders, thrilling activities, and the remarkable experiences that make it a must-visit destination for nature lovers and adventure seekers.

Introduction to Outdoor Adventures in Northern California:

Begin your journey by immersing yourself in the natural splendor and endless possibilities for outdoor exploration in Northern California. Learn about the region's diverse landscapes, including ancient forests, towering peaks, scenic coastlines, and pristine waterways. Discover the range of activities available, from hiking and camping to surfing, kayaking, and wildlife viewing. Northern California is a playground for outdoor enthusiasts, offering a wealth of adventures for all ages and skill levels.

Redwood National and State Parks:

Experience the awe-inspiring beauty of the towering redwoods in Redwood National and State Parks. Explore the ancient groves of these majestic giants, some of which are over 2,000 years old and reach heights of over 300 feet. Hike along scenic trails such as the Lady Bird Johnson Grove Trail or the Tall Trees Grove Trail, where you can marvel at the grandeur of these ancient trees. Immerse yourself in the peaceful serenity of the redwood forest and connect with nature in its most majestic form.

Yosemite National Park:

Embark on an unforgettable adventure in Yosemite National Park, a natural wonderland renowned for its towering granite cliffs, cascading waterfalls, and diverse ecosystems. Hike to the top of iconic landmarks such as Half Dome and El Capitan, where breathtaking views await. Explore the park's numerous trails, which cater to all levels of experience, and discover hidden gems such as Glacier Point and Tuolumne Meadows. Yosemite offers a wide range of outdoor activities, including rock climbing, backpacking, fishing, and wildlife watching. Immerse yourself in the raw beauty of this national park and create memories that will last a lifetime.

Lake Tahoe:

Indulge in the year-round outdoor playground that is Lake Tahoe, a stunning alpine lake nestled in the Sierra Nevada Mountains. During the summer months, enjoy water activities such as swimming, paddleboarding, and kayaking in the crystal-clear waters. Hike along the scenic trails that surround the lake, offering breathtaking vistas of the turquoise waters and surrounding peaks. In winter, Lake Tahoe transforms into a winter wonderland, inviting you to ski, snowboard, or snowshoe on the powdery slopes of its world-class ski resorts. Whether you visit in summer or winter, Lake Tahoe offers endless opportunities for outdoor adventures and unforgettable experiences.

Point Reyes National Seashore:

Discover the rugged beauty of Point Reyes National Seashore, a pristine coastal wilderness located just north of San Francisco. Hike along the coastal trails, where you can witness dramatic cliffs, secluded beaches, and panoramic ocean views. Explore the tide pools teeming with marine life, or embark on a whale-watching excursion to catch a glimpse of migrating gray whales. Point Reyes National Seashore is a paradise for birdwatchers, with over 490 species of birds recorded in the area. Immerse yourself in the untouched beauty of this coastal gem and experience the tranquility of the natural world.

Lassen Volcanic National Park:

Embark on a volcanic adventure in Lassen Volcanic National Park, a lesser-known but equally captivating national park in Northern California. Hike through otherworldly landscapes dotted with hydrothermalfeatures, including bubbling mud pots, steaming fumaroles, and colorful hot springs. Explore the park's numerous trails, where you can witness the volcanic activity up close and marvel at the unique geology. Climb to the summit of

Lassen Peak, the park's iconic volcano, for panoramic views of the surrounding landscapes. Lassen Volcanic National Park offers a fascinating blend of geology, outdoor adventure, and natural beauty.

Coastal Exploration:

Experience the rugged and breathtaking coastline of Northern California, which stretches for hundreds of miles along the Pacific Ocean. Explore scenic coastal trails, such as the Mendocino Coast Trail or the Big Sur coastline, where you can hike above dramatic cliffs and witness crashing waves. Discover hidden coves and secluded beaches where you can relax, picnic, or explore tide pools. Take a scenic drive along the Pacific Coast Highway, also known as Highway 1, where you can marvel at the stunning ocean views and stop at iconic landmarks such as Bixby Bridge and McWay Falls. Coastal exploration in Northern California is an adventure that will leave you in awe of nature's power and beauty.

Mount Shasta:

Conquer the majestic Mount Shasta, one of the tallest peaks in Northern California. Hike through alpine meadows and old-growth forests as you make your way to the summit, where breathtaking panoramic views await. Mount Shasta offers a range of hiking options, from day hikes to multi-day expeditions, catering to all levels of experience. During the winter months, Mount Shasta transforms into a winter playground, inviting you to ski, snowboard, or snowshoe on its pristine slopes. Whether you challenge yourself with a summit climb or simply admire the mountain from afar, Mount Shasta promises an outdoor adventure of epic proportions.

Trinity Alps Wilderness:

Venture into the remote and rugged wilderness of the Trinity Alps, a mountain range renowned for its breathtaking beauty and exceptional hiking opportunities. Embark on multi-day backpacking trips through alpine meadows, traverse granite peaks, and swim in pristine mountain lakes. Explore the myriad of trails that wind through the Trinity Alps Wilderness, where solitude and natural beauty await at every turn. This untouched wilderness provides a true escape into the heart of nature.

Whitewater Rafting:

Experience the thrill of whitewater rafting on the wild and scenic rivers of Northern California. From the mighty American River to the exhilarating rapids of the Trinity River and the Tuolumne River, there are options for all levels of experience. Join a guided rafting trip, where experienced guides will navigate you through the rapids and provide a safe and exciting adventure. Whitewater rafting in Northern California offers an adrenaline-pumping experience surrounded by stunning natural beauty.

Wildlife Viewing:

Northern California is home to a rich diversity

of wildlife, providing ample opportunities for wildlife viewing. Visit the Farallon Islands, located off the coast of San Francisco, to observe a variety of marine mammals, including seals, sea lions, and whales. Explore the Sacramento National Wildlife Refuge Complex, where you can spot migratory birds, waterfowl, and other wildlife in their natural habitats. Keep an eye out for bald eagles, black bears, and elusive mountain lions as you explore the wilderness areas of Northern California. Wildlife viewing in this region is a captivating and unforgettable experience.

Camping and RVing:

Immerse yourself in the great outdoors by camping or RVing in Northern California's beautiful parks and campgrounds. From beachfront campsites along the coast to forested campsites nestled among towering trees, there are options to suit every preference. Enjoy nights under the stars, gather around a campfire, and wake up to the sounds of nature. Camping and RVing allow you to fully embrace the outdoor experience, connect withthe natural world, and create lasting memories.

Northern California is a haven for outdoor adventurers, offering a diverse range of landscapes and activities that cater to every interest and skill level. Whether you seek the serenity of ancient forests, the thrill of conquering mountain peaks, the awe-inspiring beauty of the coastline, or the adrenaline rush of whitewater rafting, Northern California has it all. Immerse yourself in the natural wonders, embrace the spirit of adventure, and create unforgettable experiences in the outdoor playground of Northern California.

Hidden Gems and Off-the-Beaten-Path Destinations

Welcome to the hidden gems and off-the-beaten-path destinations of Northern California, where enchanting landscapes, cultural treasures, and unique experiences await those who dare to venture beyond the well-trodden path. While popular destinations like San Francisco and Napa Valley have their allure, Northern California is also home to a multitude of lesser-known treasures that offer a glimpse into the region's hidden beauty and rich heritage. In this chapter, we will guide you through the essence of these hidden gems and off-the-beaten-path destinations, revealing the secrets that make them special and the remarkable experiences that await intrepid travelers.

Mendocino:

Nestled along the rugged coastline, the charming town of Mendocino beckons with its picturesque beauty and artistic charm. Explore the historic downtown area, filled with unique shops, art galleries, and cozy cafes. Stroll along the breathtaking Mendocino Headlands, where you can marvel at dramatic cliffs, hidden coves, and panoramic ocean views. Visit the Mendocino Coast Botanical Gardens, showcasing a dazzling array of colorful blooms and serene landscapes. Mendocino's natural beauty, small-town charm, and artistic spirit make it a hidden gem worth discovering.

Avenue of the Giants:

Journey into the ancient realm of towering redwoods along the Avenue of the Giants. This scenic stretch of Highway 101 winds its way through Humboldt Redwoods State Park, offering a mesmerizing drive through some of the world's tallest and oldest trees. Take your time to explore the park's trails, where you can walk among giants, witness hidden waterfalls, and feel the peacefulness of the ancient forest. The Avenue of the Giants is a hidden gem that invites you to reconnect with nature and experience the magnificence of these majestic giants.

Lava Beds National Monument:

Embark on an otherworldly adventure in Lava Beds National Monument, located in the northeastern corner of California. Explore a surreal landscape shaped by volcanic activity, featuring lava tube caves, rugged lava flows, and cinder cones. Wander through the underground labyrinth of lava tube caves, marveling at unique geological formations and ancient lava beds. Learn about the rich cultural history of the area, including the presence of indigenous tribes and the Modoc War. Lava Beds National Monument offers a captivating journey into a land shaped by fire and time.

Point Arena-Stornetta Public Lands:

Discover a coastal paradise at Point Arena-Stornetta Public Lands, located along the rugged Mendocino coastline. This pristine coastal area is a haven for wildlife and offers stunning vistas of dramatic cliffs, hidden coves, and crashing waves.

Take a leisurely hike along the coastal trails, where you can spot seals, sea lions, and a variety of bird species. Marvel at the iconic Point Arena Lighthouse, perched on a rocky promontory and providing panoramic views of the Pacific Ocean. Point Arena-Stornetta Public Lands is a hidden gem where you can experience the raw beauty of the California coast.

Lost Coast:

Embark on an unforgettable adventure along the remote and rugged Lost Coast, one of the few remaining undeveloped stretches of coastline in California. This wild and untouched region is characterized by steep cliffs, pristine beaches, and a sense of isolation. Hike the Lost Coast Trail, a challenging but rewarding trek that takes you through breathtaking landscapes and provides opportunities to spot marine mammals and explore hidden coves. The Lost Coast offers a unique escape into nature, where you can disconnect from the modern world and immerse yourself in the untamed beauty of the coastline.

Anza-Borrego Desert State Park:

Venture into the desert landscapes of Anza-Borrego Desert State Park, located in Southern California but still within reachof Northern California travelers. This vast and diverse desert park showcases stunning geological formations, colorful wildflowers, and a wide array of desert flora and fauna. Explore the park's numerous hiking trails, where you can witness unique desert ecosystems, discover hidden oases, and admire towering cacti. Marvel at the vibrant wildflower blooms that blanket the desert floor during the spring months. Anza-Borrego Desert State Park offers a captivating escape into the stark beauty and tranquility of the desert.

McArthur-Burney Falls Memorial State Park:

Experience the awe-inspiring beauty of McArthur-Burney Falls Memorial State Park, home to one of California's most magnificent waterfalls. The centerpiece of the park, Burney Falls, is a 129-foot tall waterfall with a constant flow of crystal-clear water that cascades into an emerald pool. Take a leisurely stroll along the park's trails, where you can explore lush forests, serene meadows, and picturesque streams. The park also offers camping and picnic areas, allowing you to fully immerse yourself in the tranquil ambiance of this hidden gem.

Calistoga:

Escape to the relaxing and rejuvenating town of Calistoga, nestled in the northern part of Napa Valley. Known for its geothermal hot springs and mud baths, Calistoga offers a unique wellness experience. Indulge in a soothing soak in a natural hot spring or treat yourself to a luxurious spa treatment. Explore the charming downtown area, where you can find boutique shops, art galleries, and world-class restaurants. Calistoga's serene ambiance and wellness-focused offerings make it a hidden gem for those seeking relaxation and rejuvenation.

Trinidad:

Discover the coastal beauty and small-town charm of Trinidad, a picturesque village located on the Northern California coastline. With its stunning beaches, rugged cliffs, and tranquil harbor, Trinidad offers a serene and idyllic setting. Explore Trinidad State Beach, where you can stroll along sandy shores, watch for whales and seals, and witness stunning sunsets. Visit the Trinidad Museum, which showcases the rich cultural and natural history of the area. Trinidad is a hidden gem that embodies the coastal beauty and laid-back charm of Northern California.

Siskiyou County:

Escape the crowds and venture into the unspoiled wilderness of Siskiyou County, located in the far north of California. This vast and diverse region is a playground for outdoor adventurers, offering opportunities for hiking, fishing, camping, and wildlife viewing. Explore the majestic peaks of the Trinity Alps Wilderness, paddle along the pristine waters of the Klamath River, or marvel at the beauty of Mount Shasta. Siskiyou County is a hidden gem for those seeking solitude and outdoor adventures in a rugged and untouched landscape.

Ferndale:

Step back in time as you visit the charming Victorian village of Ferndale, nestled in the heart of the Lost Coast region. Explore the well-preserved historic downtown, adorned with colorful Victorian-era buildings and boutique shops. Take a leisurely stroll along Main Street, where you can find art galleries, antique stores, and delightful cafes. Discover the rich history of Ferndale at the Ferndale Museum, which showcases artifacts and exhibits that tell the story of this unique town. Ferndale's nostalgic ambiance and architectural beauty make it a hidden gem for history buffs and those seeking a glimpse into the past.

Castle Crags State Park:

Immerse yourself in the dramatic beauty of Castle Crags State Park, located in the southernmost reaches of the Cascade Range. This rugged and picturesque park is dominated by the jagged granite spires of Castle Crags, which rise dramatically above the surrounding forests. Hike along the park's trails, which offer stunning vistas of the crags, lush meadows,and the Sacramento River. Explore the Castle Crags Wilderness, a designated wilderness area within the park, where you can discover hidden lakes, alpine meadows, and pristine forests. Castle Crags State Park is a hidden gem that provides a peaceful and awe-inspiring escape into nature's grandeur.

Northern California is a treasure trove of hidden gems and off-the-beaten-path destinations, offering unique experiences and the chance to discover lesser-known corners of this captivating region. Venture beyond the familiar and embrace the allure of these hidden gems, where you can connect with nature, immerse yourself in local culture, and create memories that will last a lifetime. These hidden treasures are waiting to be explored by those who seek a truly authentic and off-the-beaten-path Northern California experience.

Exploring Northern California's Art and Cultural Scene

Welcome to the vibrant and diverse art and cultural scene of Northern California, where creativity, innovation, and a rich heritage converge. From world-class museums and galleries to captivating performing arts venues and cultural festivals, Northern California offers a wealth of opportunities to immerse yourself in artistic expression and discover the region's unique cultural identity. In this chapter, we will guide you through the essence of Northern California's art and cultural scene, showcasing the notable institutions, events, and experiences that make it a must-visit destination for art lovers and culture enthusiasts.

San Francisco Museum of Modern Art (SFMOMA):

Begin your journey into Northern California's art scene at SFMOMA, one of the largest modern and contemporary art museums in the country. Explore a vast collection of artworks spanning different mediums and styles, from painting and sculpture to photography, video, and performance art. SFMOMA showcases works by renowned artists such as Jackson Pollock, Frida Kahlo, and Andy Warhol, as well as emerging contemporary artists. Immerse yourself in thought-provoking exhibitions, attend artist talks and lectures, and experience the ever-evolving world of modern and contemporary art.

de Young Museum:

Located in San Francisco's Golden Gate Park, the de Young Museum is a haven for art enthusiasts and cultural explorers. Discover a diverse collection of American art from the 17th through the 21st centuries, as well as art from Africa, Oceania, and the Americas. Marvel at iconic works, such as Albert Bierstadt's "Among the Sierra Nevada Mountains" and Georgia O'Keeffe's "The Lawrence Tree." The de Young Museum also hosts rotating exhibitions that showcase a wide range of artistic styles and movements. Don't miss the opportunity to climb to the museum's observation deck, where you can enjoy panoramic views of the city and the park.

Crocker Art Museum:

Venture to Sacramento and visit the Crocker Art Museum, the longest continuously operating art museum in the West. Explore an impressive collection of California art, European masterpieces, and international ceramics. The museum's historic building, a blend of Victorian and Italianate architecture, adds to the charm of the experience. Take part in educational programs, workshops, and guided tours that provide insights into the artworks and the region's artistic heritage. The Crocker Art Museum is a cultural gem that showcases the beauty and diversity of artistic expression.

Contemporary Jewish Museum:

Delve into Jewish culture and contemporary

art at the Contemporary Jewish Museum in San Francisco. Discover thought-provoking exhibitions that explore Jewish history, art, and identity. The museum presents a dynamic mix of contemporary art, multimedia installations, and engaging educational programs. Explore themes of social justice, spirituality, and cultural diversity through the lens of Jewish heritage. The Contemporary Jewish Museum offers a unique and thought-provoking experience that bridges art, culture, and identity.

Exploratorium:

Immerse yourself in the intersection of art, science, and human perception at the Exploratorium in San Francisco. This interactive museum is a playground for curious minds of all ages, offering a hands-on exploration of scientific phenomena and artistic expression. Engage with exhibits that challenge your senses, spark creativity, and encourage active participation. From the Tactile Dome, where you navigate a pitch-black environment by touch, to the outdoor exhibits that take advantage of the beautiful waterfront location, the Exploratorium fosters a deep appreciation for the art and science of the world around us.

Native American Art and Culture:

Discover the rich artistic traditions and cultural heritage of Northern California's Native American tribes. Visit the California Indian Museum and Cultural Center in Santa Rosa, which celebrates the diverse cultures of California's indigenous peoples through exhibitions, workshops, and educational programs. Explore the Grace Hudson Museum in Ukiah, dedicated to preserving and showcasing the art and artifacts of the Pomo people. Attend powwows and cultural events held by various tribes throughout the region, where you can experience traditional dances, music, and crafts. Northern California provides a unique opportunity to connect with and appreciate the rich artistic and cultural legacies of Native American communities.

Shakespearean Theater:

Experience the magic of live theater at the renowned Oregon Shakespeare Festival in Ashland, just across the border in Oregon. This world-class theater festival presents a diverse repertoire of Shakespearean plays, classic works, and contemporary productions. Immerse yourself in the enchanting atmosphere of the outdoor Elizabethan Theatre, where the works of Shakespeare come to life against the backdrop of nature. Explore the festival's multiple stages and diverse performances, including modern adaptations and new works. The Oregon Shakespeare Festival offers a captivating blend of artistry, storytelling, and theatrical innovation.

Cultural Festivals:

Celebrate the region's vibrant cultural diversity by attending one of Northern California's many cultural festivals. From the Chinese New

Year Parade in San Francisco's Chinatown to the Solano Stroll, a multicultural extravaganza in Berkeley, these festivals showcase the traditions, cuisines, music, and dances of various ethnic communities. Explore the Greek Festival in Sacramento, the Cinco de Mayo celebrations in the Central Valley, or the Santa Cruz Greek Cultural Festival. Immerse yourself in the lively atmosphere, try international delicacies, and appreciate the beauty of cultural exchange.

Street Art and Murals:

Experience the vibrant street art scene that graces the walls of many Northern California cities. Take a stroll through San Francisco's Mission District, where colorful murals adorn buildings, telling stories of community, social justice, and cultural heritage. Explore the vibrant street art scene in Oakland's Uptown neighborhood, where local artists express their creativity through murals and graffiti art. Discover the ever-evolving street art in Sacramento's Midtown district, where you can witness the transformation of public spaces into open-air galleries. Northern California's street art reflects the region's diverse cultural landscape and serves as a platform for self-expression and social commentary.

Music and Performing Arts:

Immerse yourself in the region's thriving music and performing arts scene. Attend a symphony performance by the San Francisco

Symphony or the Sacramento Philharmonic & Opera, where world-class musicians bring classical masterpieces to life. Explore the jazz clubs of San Francisco's Fillmore District or the vibrant live music scene in Sacramento's Midtown. Experience the joy of live theater and dance at venues such as the California Theatre in San Jose, the Crest Theatre in Sacramento, or the Luther Burbank Center for the Arts in Santa Rosa. Northern California offers a diverse range of musical genres and performing arts, ensuring there's something to suit every taste.

Art Walks and Open Studios:

Engage with local artists and explore their creative spaces during art walks and open studio events. Visit San Francisco's First Thursday Art Walk in the vibrant Mission District, where galleries open their doors to showcase the works of emerging and established artists. Discover the Open Studios events held throughout the region, such as the East Bay Open Studios or the Silicon Valley Open Studios, where you can meet artists in their studios, learn about their artistic processes, and purchase unique artworks. These events offer a glimpse into the local art scene and provide an opportunity to support and connect with talented artists.

Literary Heritage:

Discover the literary heritage of Northern California, a region that has inspired numerous writers and poets. Visit the Beat Museum in San

Francisco's North Beach neighborhood, dedicated to the Beat Generation and its literary figures such as Jack Kerouac and Allen Ginsberg. Explore the John Steinbeck House in Salinas, wherethe Nobel Prize-winning author spent his childhood and drew inspiration for his iconic works. Attend literary events and book festivals, such as the Litquake Festival in San Francisco or the Sacramento Poetry Center's reading series, where you can engage with local and visiting authors. Northern California's literary heritage is alive and thriving, offering a glimpse into the creative minds that have shaped the region's cultural landscape.

Northern California's art and cultural scene is a testament to the region's vibrant creativity, rich history, and diverse communities. Immerse yourself in the world-class museums, galleries, and cultural events that showcase the artistic expressions of the past and present. Engage with the local arts community, explore hidden corners of creativity, and celebrate the region's unique cultural tapestry. Northern California offers a rich and dynamic cultural experience that will leave you inspired, enriched, and craving for more.

Family-Friendly Activities in Northern California

Welcome to Northern California, a region that offers a wealth of family-friendly activities and attractions to delight travelers of all ages. From interactive museums and theme parks to outdoor adventures and educational experiences, Northern California is a perfect destination for a memorable family vacation. In this chapter, we will guide you through the essence of family-friendly activities in Northern California, highlighting the top attractions and experiences that will create lasting memories for your family.

Exploratorium:

Ignite your curiosity and engage in hands-on learning at the Exploratorium in San Francisco. This interactive science museum offers a wide range of exhibits that explore the wonders of physics, biology, art, and more. From building circuits and experimenting with light and sound to exploring the human body and the natural world, the Exploratorium provides endless opportunities for discovery and exploration. The museum's emphasis on hands-on experiences and interactive exhibits makes it a hit with children and adults alike.

California Academy of Sciences:

Embark on a journey of scientific exploration at the California Academy of Sciences in San Francisco's Golden Gate Park. This unique institution combines a natural history museum, aquarium, planetarium, and rainforest exhibit all under one roof. Get up close to diverse marine life at the aquarium, gaze at the stars in the planetarium, and explore the rainforest exhibit with its lush foliage and exotic creatures. The California Academy of Sciences offers a captivating and educational experience for the whole family.

Children's Creativity Museum:

Unleash your child's creativity and imagination at the Children's Creativity Museum in San Francisco. This interactive museum focuses on fostering innovation, collaboration, and problem-solving skills through various exhibits and activities. Kids can design their own digital animations, create music using virtual instruments, and explore the world of storytelling through digital media. The museum's emphasis on creativity and technology makes it a unique and engaging experience for young minds.

California's Great America:

Experience thrilling rides and family entertainment at California's Great America, a popular amusement park located in Santa Clara. With a wide range of rides, including roller coasters, water slides, and live shows, there's something for everyone in the family to enjoy. From adrenaline-pumping coasters like RailBlazer to family-friendly attractions like Planet Snoopy, California's Great America offers a day of fun and excitement for all ages.

Six Flags Discovery Kingdom:

Embark on an unforgettable adventure at Six Flags Discovery Kingdom in Vallejo. This unique theme park combines thrilling rides with up-close animal encounters. Experience the adrenaline rush of roller coasters and water slides, and then immerse yourself in the animal exhibits and shows, where you can see dolphins, sea lions, tigers, and more. Six Flags Discovery Kingdom offers a diverse range of experiences that will entertain the whole family.

Monterey Bay Aquarium:

Dive into the wonders of the ocean at the Monterey Bay Aquarium, located on Cannery Row in Monterey. Explore fascinating exhibits that showcase a diverse array of marine life, from playful sea otters and mesmerizing jellyfish to majestic sharks and colorful coral reefs. Participate in educational programs and interactive exhibits that promote conservation and environmental awareness. The Monterey Bay Aquarium offers a captivating and educational experience that will leave a lasting impression on visitors of all ages.

California State Railroad Museum:

All aboard! Step back in time at the California State Railroad Museum in Sacramento, where you can explore the history and impact of the railroad on California's development. Discover beautifully restored locomotives, historic railcars, and interactive exhibits that showcase the golden age of rail travel. Kids will love climbing aboard the full-size steam locomotives and exploring the hands-on exhibits that bring the history of the railroad to life.

Oakland Zoo:

Embark on a wild adventure at the Oakland Zoo, home to a wide array of animals from around the world. Explore the zoo's exhibits, which feature elephants, giraffes, lions, tigers, and many other fascinating creatures. The zoo also offers interactive activities, such as the Outback Express Adventure Train and the Sky Ride, providing unique perspectives and experiences for visitors of all ages. The Oakland Zoo is a family-friendly destination that combines education, conservation, and fun.

Santa Cruz Beach Boardwalk:

Head to Santa Cruz and experience the classic seaside amusement park, Santa Cruz Beach Boardwalk. Take a ride on the historic Giant Dipper roller coaster, enjoy classic carnival games, and indulge in delicious treats like cotton candy and funnel cakes. The beachfront location provides an opportunity for kids to build sandcastles, fly kites, and splash in the waves. With its nostalgic charm and family-friendly attractions, the Santa Cruz Beach Boardwalk offers a day of old-fashioned fun and entertainment.

Sacramento Zoo:

Discover the wonders of the animal kingdom at the Sacramento Zoo, located in William Land Park. Explore the zoo's exhibits, which house a variety of animals, including primates, reptiles, birds, and big cats. Participate in animal feedings and keeper talks to learn more about the zoo's residents and their habitats. The Sacramento Zoo offers a relaxed and intimate setting, making it a great destination for families with young children.

Jelly Belly Factory Tour:

Take a behind-the-scenes tour of the Jelly Belly Factory in Fairfield and discover the secrets behind these iconic jelly beans. Witness the bean-making process, learn about the flavors, and taste a variety of jelly bean flavors during the tour. Kids will love the interactive exhibits and the opportunity to sample different flavors. The Jelly Belly Factory Tour provides a sweet and enjoyable experience for the whole family.

Outdoor Adventures:

Northern California's natural beauty provides ample opportunities for outdoor adventures that the whole family can enjoy. Explore the majestic redwoods in Muir Woods National Monument, where easy trails allow for leisurely walks amidst towering trees. Discover the beauty of Lake Tahoe and engage in activities such as hiking, biking, and paddleboarding. Visit one of the region's many state parks, such as Armstrong Redwoods State Natural Reserve or Pinnacles National Park, for opportunities to hike, picnic, and observe wildlife. Outdoor adventures in Northern California offer a chance to connect with nature and create unforgettable family memories.

Northern California is a treasure trove of

family-friendly activities and attractions that cater to the interests and curiosity of travelers of all ages. Whether you're exploring interactive museums, enjoying thrilling amusement park rides, or embarking on outdoor adventures, the region offers a diverse range of experiences that will create lasting memories for your family. Embrace the magic of Northern California and enjoy a vacation filled with laughter, exploration, and quality time together.

Epic Road Trips: Discovering Northern California by Car

Northern California is a road tripper's dream, with its breathtaking landscapes, iconic highways, and a multitude of hidden gems waiting to be discovered. Embarking on a road trip is the perfect way to explore the diverse regions of Northern California, from the rugged coastline to the towering redwoods, from the vibrant cities to the tranquil countryside. In this chapter, we will guide you through epic road trips that showcase the best of Northern California, allowing you to create unforgettable memories and experience the freedom of the open road.

Pacific Coast Highway (Highway 1):

One of the most iconic road trips in the world, driving along the Pacific Coast Highway is a must for any Northern California itinerary. Starting in San Francisco, follow Highway 1 south, hugging the coastline as you pass through charming coastal towns like Santa Cruz, Monterey, and Carmel-by-the-Sea. Marvel at the dramatic cliffs, sandy beaches, and panoramic ocean views along the way. Don't miss the opportunity to visit the famous Bixby Bridge and explore the natural beauty of Big Sur. The Pacific Coast Highway offers a scenic and unforgettable journey along California's stunning coastline.

Redwood National and State Parks Loop:

Immerse yourself in the enchanting world of the towering redwoods on this road trip through

Northern California's Redwood National and State Parks. Begin your journey in Crescent City and head south on Highway 101, where you'll be surrounded by ancient giants in Jedediah Smith Redwoods State Park and Prairie Creek Redwoods State Park. Continue on to the Avenue of the Giants, a scenic byway that winds through Humboldt Redwoods State Park. Make sure to stop and explore the numerous trails, picnic areas, and visitor centers along the way. This road trip offers a truly awe-inspiring experience as you drive through the majestic redwood forests.

Sierra Nevada Loop:

Embark on a journey through the stunning Sierra Nevada mountains on this scenic road trip. Start in Sacramento and head east on Highway 50, passing through charming towns like Placerville and South Lake Tahoe. Enjoy the picturesque beauty of Lake Tahoe and its surrounding mountains before continuing south on Highway 395. Explore the quaint towns of Bishop and Lone Pine, where you can admire the towering peaks of the Eastern Sierra, including Mount Whitney, the highest point in the contiguous United States. Take your time to enjoy outdoor activities like hiking, fishing, and photography along this breathtaking route.

Gold Country Adventure:

Discover the rich history of California's Gold Rush era on this road trip through the picturesque towns of Gold Country. Start in Sacramento and follow Highway 49, winding through charming towns like Placerville, Nevada City, and Sonora. Explore historic sites, visit museums, and try your hand at gold panning. Immerse yourself in the stories of the past as you stroll through the preserved streets of towns that still maintain their 19th-century charm. Don't forget to sample local wines in the renowned vineyards of the Sierra Foothills. This road trip offers a fascinating journey back in time and a chance to experience the spirit of the Gold Rush.

Volcanic Wonders:

Embark on a road trip through Northern California's volcanic landscape, where you can witness the remnants of ancient eruptions and explore unique geological features. Start in Redding and head east on Highway 299 to Lassen Volcanic National Park. Marvel at the bubbling mud pots, steaming fumaroles, and the majestic peak of Lassen Peak. Continue south on Highway 89 and visit the impressive volcanic formations of McArthur-Burney Falls Memorial State Park. Explore the dramatic lava tube caves in Lava Beds National Monument and learn about the region's volcanic history. Thisroad trip offers a captivating journey through Northern California's volcanic wonders.

Mendocino Coastal Drive:

Experience the rugged beauty of the Northern California coastline on this scenic road trip along Highway 1. Start in the charming town of

Mendocino and drive north, soaking in the breathtaking views of the Pacific Ocean. Marvel at the towering cliffs, secluded beaches, and picturesque coastal towns along the way. Stop at Point Arena Lighthouse, where you can climb to the top for panoramic ocean views. Continue north to Fort Bragg and visit Glass Beach, known for its sparkling sea glass treasures. The Mendocino Coastal Drive offers a peaceful and scenic escape along one of the most stunning coastlines in the world.

Wine Country Escape:

Indulge in the flavors of Northern California's wine country on this road trip through Napa and Sonoma Valleys. Start in Napa and follow Highway 29, passing through vineyards and wineries that offer tastings and tours. Explore the charming towns of Yountville, St. Helena, and Calistoga, where you can enjoy world-class cuisine and luxurious spas. Cross over to Sonoma Valley and continue your journey through picturesque vineyards and rolling hills. Visit the historic Sonoma Plaza and enjoy the laid-back atmosphere of this renowned wine region. The Wine Country Escape road trip is a perfect blend of scenic beauty, culinary delights, and wine tasting experiences.

Shasta Cascade Adventure:

Embark on an outdoor adventure through the magnificent landscapes of the Shasta Cascade region on this road trip. Start in Redding and head north on Interstate 5 to Shasta Lake, where you can enjoy boating, fishing, and hiking in the surrounding Shasta-Trinity National Forest. Continue east on Highway 299 and explore the stunning waterfalls and trails of McCloud and Burney Falls. Journey further east to Lassen Volcanic National Park and witness the park's volcanic wonders. End your trip by visiting the picturesque town of Mount Shasta, nestled at the base of the majestic Mount Shasta. The Shasta Cascade Adventure offers a diverse range of outdoor activities and breathtaking scenery.

Avenue of the Giants:

Immerse yourself in the magic of the ancient redwoods on this road trip along the Avenue of the Giants. Start in Garberville and drive south on the scenic Avenue of the Giants, a 31-mile stretch of road that runs parallel to Highway 101. Marvel at the towering redwoods that line the route and explore the numerous scenic viewpoints and hiking trails along the way. Visit the Humboldt Redwoods State Park Visitor Center for information and exhibits about the region's redwood forests. The Avenue of the Giants road trip offers a tranquil and awe-inspiring journey through some of the world's tallest trees.

Lake Tahoe Circle Tour:

Experience the natural beauty of Lake Tahoe on this road trip that takes you around the entire lake. Start in South Lake Tahoe and drive along the eastern shore, passing through charming towns like Incline Village and Kings Beach. Enjoy panoramic lake views and stop at hidden beaches along the way. Continue along the western shore, where you can visit Emerald Bay State Park and hike to the stunning Vikingsholm Castle. Drive through quaint towns like Tahoe City and Homewood before completing the circle back to South Lake Tahoe. The Lake Tahoe Circle Tour showcases the crystal-clear waters, majestic mountains, and picturesque towns that make this region a popular destination.

Sacramento River Scenic Drive:

Discover the beauty of the Sacramento River on this scenic drive that follows the river's course through Northern California. Start in Sacramento and head north on Interstate 5, enjoying the views of the river and the surrounding countryside. Pass through charming towns like Colusa, Chico, and Red Bluff, where you can explore historic downtown areas and enjoy riveractivities such as boating and fishing. Take detours to visit wildlife refuges and state parks along the way, where you can spot birds, hike nature trails, and enjoy picnic areas. The Sacramento River Scenic Drive offers a serene and picturesque journey through the heart of Northern California.

Lost Coast Adventure:

Embark on a road trip to the remote and rugged beauty of the Lost Coast, a stretch of coastline untouched by major development. Start in Ferndale and head west on Mattole Road, which winds through the scenic King Range National Conservation Area. Take your time to explore the hidden coves, pristine beaches, and towering cliffs that define this unique region. Hike a portion of the Lost Coast Trail, where you can experience the solitude and breathtaking views of the Pacific Ocean. The Lost Coast Adventure road trip offers a truly off-the-beaten-path experience in one of California's most stunning and untouched coastal areas.

Northern California's epic road trips offer a diverse range of landscapes, attractions, and experiences that cater to every traveler's interests. From coastal drives to mountain adventures, from wine country escapes to historical journeys, each road trip presents an opportunity to discover the region's unique charm and natural beauty. So, grab your keys, buckle up, and get ready to embark on an unforgettable journey through Northern California's scenic highways and hidden treasures.

Exploring Northern California's Coastal Cuisine

Northern California's coastal region is not only known for its stunning beaches and breathtaking views but also for its vibrant and diverse culinary scene. From fresh seafood and farm-to-table delights to award-winning wineries and artisanal food producers, the coastal cuisine of Northern California offers a feast for the senses. In this chapter, we will take you on a culinary journey, introducing you to the unique flavors, local ingredients, and iconic dishes that make Northern California's coastal cuisine a must-experience for food enthusiasts and travelers alike.

Dungeness Crab:

One of the signature dishes of Northern California's coastal cuisine is Dungeness crab. Known for its sweet and succulent meat, Dungeness crab is a local delicacy that can be enjoyed in a variety of ways. From freshly steamed whole crabs served with melted butter to crab cakes, crab bisque, and crab louie salad, there are countless ways to savor this delectable crustacean. Visit local seafood markets and restaurants along the coast to experience the best of Dungeness crab during the peak season, which typically runs from November to June.

Oysters:

Northern California's pristine coastal waters provide an ideal environment for growing oysters, and the region is renowned for its oyster farms and fresh shucked oysters. Whether you prefer them raw on the half-shell, grilled, or baked in a savory dish, you'll find an abundance of options to satisfy your oyster cravings. Head to the historic town of Tomales Bay, where you can visit oyster farms and enjoy oysters with a side of scenic beauty. Hog Island Oyster Co. and Tomales Bay Oyster Co. are just a couple of the notable oyster destinations in the area.

Cioppino:

A classic seafood stew that originated in San Francisco, cioppino is a must-try dish when exploring Northern California's coastal cuisine. This hearty and flavorful stew typically features a medley of seafood such as Dungeness crab, clams, mussels, shrimp, and various types of fish cooked in a tomato-based broth infused with aromatic herbs and spices. Enjoy a bowl of cioppino with crusty sourdough bread, and you'll savor the rich flavors of the sea. Many seafood restaurants in San Francisco and other coastal towns offer their own variations of this beloved dish.

Artisanal Cheese:

Northern California's coastal region is home to numerous artisanal cheese producers who take pride in crafting high-quality cheeses from locally sourced ingredients. From creamy goat cheeses and tangy blue cheeses to aged cheddars and nutty Goudas, there's a cheese for every palate. Visit cheese shops and creameries in towns like Point Reyes Station and Petaluma to sample a wide range of artisanal cheeses. Don't miss the opportunity to taste the famous Point Reyes Original Blue, Cowgirl Creamery's Mt. Tam, and other award-winning cheeses that showcase the region's dairy heritage.

Farm-to-Table Delights:

Northern California's coastal cuisine celebrates the abundance of fresh, locally grown produce. The region's fertile farmlands and mild climate allow for a wide variety of fruits, vegetables, and herbs to thrive. Many restaurants embrace the farm-to-table philosophy, sourcing ingredients directly from local farms and incorporating them into their dishes. Indulge in vibrant salads made with seasonal greens, enjoy farm-fresh heirloom tomatoes, and savor dishes that highlight the flavors of locally sourced produce. The freshness and quality of the ingredients elevate the dining experience and connect you to the region's agricultural roots.

Wine and Wine Country Cuisine:

The coastal region of Northern California is home to some of the country's most renowned wineries and vineyards. From the rolling hills of Napaand Sonoma to the Anderson Valley and Santa Cruz Mountains, the coastal wine regions offer not only exceptional wines but also a culinary experience that perfectly complements the local vintages. Many wineries feature on-site restaurants, where you can enjoy farm-to-table cuisine paired with their wines. Indulge in wine country cuisine, which emphasizes locally sourced ingredients, seasonal flavors, and innovative culinary techniques. From wine tastings and vineyard tours to wine-paired meals, the coastal wine regions provide an immersive and delightful culinary experience.

Farmers Markets and Local Produce:

Immerse yourself in the vibrant local food scene by visiting farmers markets along the coast. From the renowned Ferry Plaza Farmers Market in San Francisco to smaller markets in coastal towns, these gatherings showcase the region's abundance of fresh produce, artisanal products, and gourmet treats. Stroll through the market stalls, sample seasonal fruits and vegetables, pick up artisan cheeses, freshly baked bread, and locally made preserves. Interacting with local farmers and food producers offers a deeper connection to the coastal culinary culture and a chance to support the local economy.

Sustainable Seafood:

Given the region's proximity to the Pacific Ocean, it's no surprise that sustainable seafood plays a significant role in Northern California's coastal cuisine. Many restaurants and seafood markets prioritize sustainable fishing practices and support local fishermen who follow responsible harvesting methods. Look for labels such as "Certified Sustainable Seafood" or ask for recommendations at seafood establishments to ensure you're enjoying seafood that is both delicious and harvested with the environment in mind. By choosing sustainable seafood, you contribute to the preservation of the coastal ecosystem.

Coastal Bakeries and Pastries:

No culinary exploration of Northern California's coastal cuisine is complete without indulging in the region's delectable baked goods. From flaky croissants and buttery pastries to crusty bread and decadent desserts, coastal bakeries offer a tempting array of treats. Try the iconic sourdough bread, a San Francisco specialty known for its tangy flavor and distinctive texture. Treat yourself to a slice of marionberry pie, a local favorite in Mendocino. Explore local bakeries and pastry shops along the coast, where you can savor the craftsmanship and creativity of talented bakers.

Craft Breweries and Distilleries:

Northern California's coastal region is also known for its thriving craft beer and spirits scene. Local breweries and distilleries produce a wide range of flavorful beers, ales, ciders, and spirits that reflect the region's creativity and commitment to quality. Take a brewery tour, visit tasting rooms, and sample unique brews infused with local ingredients. Craft distilleries offer a chance to taste artisanal spirits made from locally sourced grains, fruits, and botanicals. Whether you're a beer aficionado or a spirits connoisseur, exploring the coastal breweries and distilleries is a delightful way to experience the region's craft beverage culture.

Northern California's coastal cuisine showcases the region's bountiful offerings from land and sea, with a focus on fresh, locally sourced ingredients and a commitment to sustainability and quality. From Dungeness crab to artisanal cheese, farm-to-table delights to coastal wines, the culinary experiences along the coast are a true reflection of the region's natural beauty and cultural heritage. Embark on a culinary adventure and let your taste buds explore the flavors of Northern California's coastal cuisine.

Outdoor Recreation in Northern California: Hiking, Biking, and More

Northern California is a haven for outdoor enthusiasts, offering a wide range of recreational activities that take advantage of the region's diverse landscapes and natural beauty. From towering mountains and ancient redwood forests to scenic coastal trails and picturesque lakes, there are endless opportunities to explore and enjoy the great outdoors. In this chapter, we will guide you through the top outdoor recreational activities in Northern California, showcasing the best hiking trails, biking routes, and more, ensuring that you make the most of your outdoor adventures.

Hiking:

Northern California is a hiker's paradise, boasting an extensive network of trails that cater to all skill levels. Whether you're seeking a leisurely stroll through ancient redwoods or a challenging summit hike, there's a trail for you. Explore the iconic trails of Yosemite National Park, such as the Mist Trail to Vernal and Nevada Falls or the Half Dome hike for a thrilling adventure. Discover the beauty of the Lost Coast Trail, where rugged coastal cliffs meet pristine beaches. Traverse the breathtaking landscapes of the Trinity Alps Wilderness or the Lassen Volcanic National Park. Lace up your hiking boots and get ready to explore the wonders of Northern California on foot.

Biking:

Northern California offers a plethora of biking

opportunities, from scenic road cycling routes to thrilling mountain bike trails. Pedal along the Pacific Coast Highway, soaking in the coastal views and enjoying the fresh sea breeze. Traverse the rolling hills and vineyards of the Napa and Sonoma valleys, stopping at wineries along the way. For mountain bikers, explore the rugged trails of Downieville or the world-class mountain biking destination of Lake Tahoe's Northstar Bike Park. Whether you're a road cyclist or a mountain biking enthusiast, Northern California's diverse terrain provides endless options for unforgettable biking adventures.

Water Sports:

With its abundance of lakes, rivers, and the Pacific Ocean, Northern California offers a wealth of water sports and activities. Explore the pristine waters of Lake Tahoe and enjoy paddleboarding, kayaking, or sailing. Experience the thrill of white-water rafting on the American River or the Trinity River. Surf the waves at popular coastal destinations such as Santa Cruz or Half Moon Bay. Go fishing in one of the many lakes and rivers teeming with trout, salmon, and bass. Northern California's waterways provide endless opportunities for water sports enthusiasts of all levels.

Camping and RVing:

Immerse yourself in the beauty of Northern California's natural landscapes by embarking on a camping or RV adventure. The region offers a wide range of campgrounds and RV parks that cater to different preferences, from remote wilderness campsites to family-friendly campgrounds with amenities. Set up camp amidst the towering redwoods in Jedediah Smith Redwoods State Park, enjoy beachfront camping along the coast, or find serenity in the mountains of the Sierra Nevada. Fall asleep under a star-filled sky, wake up to the sound of birds chirping, and create lasting memories around a campfire.

Rock Climbing:

For adrenaline seekers, Northern California offers exceptional rock climbing opportunities. The granite walls of Yosemite Valley provide world-class climbing routes for all levels of experience. Scale the iconic El Capitan or challenge yourself on the multi-pitch routes of Tuolumne Meadows. Other popular rock climbing destinations include Castle Crags State Park, Joshua Tree National Park, and Lover's Leap near Lake Tahoe. Whether you're a seasoned climber or a beginner, Northern California's diverse range of climbing spots will satisfy your craving for adventure.

Wildlife Viewing and Birdwatching:

Northern California is home to a rich diversity of wildlife, making it a paradise for nature lovers and birdwatchers. Explore the wetlands and marshes of the Sacramento-San JoaquinDelta, where you can observe a variety of bird species, including herons, egrets, and waterfowl. Visit the

Klamath Basin National Wildlife Refuges, known for their abundant bird populations, including bald eagles and pelicans. In Point Reyes National Seashore, keep an eye out for tule elk and harbor seals. Wildlife enthusiasts will also enjoy the chance to spot whales along the coast, particularly during the annual migration seasons. Grab your binoculars and camera, and get ready to witness the beauty of Northern California's wildlife.

Scenic Drives:

Take in the breathtaking vistas and scenic beauty of Northern California by embarking on a leisurely scenic drive. The Pacific Coast Highway (Highway 1) offers stunning coastal views as it winds along the rugged coastline. Journey through the iconic Avenue of the Giants, where towering redwoods create a magical canopy over the road. Explore the volcanic landscapes of Lassen Volcanic National Park on the Lassen Volcanic National Park Highway. The Cascade Lakes Scenic Byway showcases the picturesque beauty of the Shasta Cascade region. Sit back, relax, and enjoy the stunning landscapes unfolding before your eyes.

Winter Sports:

When winter arrives, Northern California transforms into a winter wonderland, offering a range of winter sports activities. Hit the slopes at world-class ski resorts such as Squaw Valley, Heavenly, and Mammoth Mountain. Enjoy cross-country skiing or snowshoeing through the snow-covered landscapes of the Sierra Nevada. Try your hand at snowboarding, sledding, or tubing for a fun-filled day with family and friends. Northern California's winter sports destinations provide ample opportunities to embrace the snowy season and enjoy the thrill of cold-weather activities.

National and State Parks:

Northern California is home to numerous national and state parks that showcase the region's natural beauty and provide a playground for outdoor enthusiasts. Explore the towering granite cliffs, cascading waterfalls, and meadows of Yosemite National Park. Discover the pristine beaches, coastal dunes, and lush forests of Redwood National and State Parks. Hike through the wildflower-filled meadows and alpine landscapes of Lassen Volcanic National Park. Each park offers unique recreational opportunities, including hiking, camping, picnicking, and wildlife viewing. Embrace the outdoors and connect with nature in these protected and majestic landscapes.

Off-Roading:

For those seeking a rugged and adventurous experience, Northern California offers opportunities for off-roading and exploring remote and challenging terrains. Head to the Rubicon Trail, known as one of the most iconic off-road trails in the country, located in the Sierra Nevada near Lake Tahoe. Test your skills and maneuver through the challenging obstacles of the trail, surrounded by stunning scenery. Other popular off-roading areas include the Carnegie State Vehicular Recreation Area and the Oceano Dunes State Vehicular Recreation Area. Strap in and embark on an off-roading adventure that will get your adrenaline pumping.

Northern California's outdoor recreational opportunities are as diverse as its landscapes. Whether you're hiking through ancient redwoods, biking along scenic routes, enjoying water sports, camping under the stars, or seeking adventure in rock climbing or off-roading, the region offers endless possibilities for outdoor enthusiasts. So, lace up your boots, hop on your bike, or grab your gear, and get ready to embark on unforgettable outdoor adventures in Northern California.

Northern California's Wildlife and Nature Reserves

Northern California is blessed with an abundance of natural beauty and diverse ecosystems that provide a habitat for a wide array of wildlife species. From majestic redwood forests to pristine coastal areas, rugged mountains, and sprawling wetlands, the region offers a haven for nature lovers and wildlife enthusiasts. In this chapter, we will explore some of the remarkable wildlife and nature reserves in Northern California, where you can immerse yourself in the wonders of nature and witness the rich biodiversity that calls this region home.

Redwood National and State Parks:

One of the most iconic natural attractions in Northern California, the Redwood National and State Parks encompass a vast area of ancient redwood forests. These towering trees, some of which are over 2,000 years old and reach heights of over 300 feet, create a mystical and awe-inspiring environment. The parks provide a habitat for a variety of wildlife, including Roosevelt elk, black bears, gray foxes, and a myriad of bird species. Explore the numerous trails that wind through the forests, such as the Lady Bird Johnson Grove Trail and the Tall Trees Grove Trail, where you can witness the grandeur of the redwoods and encounter wildlife along the way.

Point Reyes National Seashore:

Located on a peninsula along the coast of

Marin County, Point Reyes National Seashore is a haven for both land and marine wildlife. The rugged coastline, sandy beaches, and lush coastal meadows provide a diverse range of habitats. Keep an eye out for tule elk, which can be spotted grazing in the grasslands. Explore the tidal pools and tidepools along the coastline, home to a variety of marine life, including starfish, anemones, and sea urchins. The seashore is also a popular spot for birdwatching, with over 490 bird species recorded in the area. From the iconic Point Reyes Lighthouse to the stunning landscapes of Drakes Beach and Chimney Rock, Point Reyes offers a wealth of opportunities to immerse yourself in nature and observe wildlife.

Sacramento National Wildlife Refuge Complex:

The Sacramento National Wildlife Refuge Complex consists of several wildlife refuges, including the Sacramento National Wildlife Refuge and the Colusa National Wildlife Refuge. These wetlands and marshes provide crucial habitat for migratory birds along the Pacific Flyway. Thousands of waterfowl, including snow geese, tundra swans, and various species of ducks, make their home in these refuges during the winter months. The complex also supports a diverse range of wildlife, such as river otters, beavers, and a variety of reptiles and amphibians. Explore the refuge trails and auto routes, where you can observe and photograph the abundant birdlife and immerse yourself in the tranquility of these natural wetlands.

Mono Lake:

Located east of the Sierra Nevada, Mono Lake is a unique and ecologically significant body of water. The lake's high salinity and alkaline conditions create a habitat for unique species, including brine shrimp and alkali flies. These tiny organisms, in turn, attract a large number of migratory birds, making Mono Lake a vital stopover for many bird species. Witness the mesmerizing tufa formations, calcium carbonate towers that rise from the lake's surface, and explore the boardwalk trails that provide access to prime birdwatching areas. Mono Lake's otherworldly beauty and importance as a habitat make it a must-visit destination for nature lovers and birdwatchers.

Sierra Nevada Mountains:

The Sierra Nevada Mountains, stretching across much of Eastern California, are a natural wonderland that provides a habitat for a diverse range of wildlife. Explore the alpine meadows and granite peaks of Yosemite National Park, where you may spot black bears, mule deer, andeven elusive mountain lions. Venture into the backcountry of the Sierra Nevada and you may encounter golden eagles soaring overhead or catch a glimpse of the rare Sierra Nevada bighorn sheep. The mountains are also home to a variety of smaller animals, such as squirrels, chipmunks, and pikas. Explore the numerous trails and wilderness areas, such as the John Muir Trail or the Desolation Wilderness, and immerse yourself in the breathtaking beauty of the Sierra Nevada while encountering the wildlife that thrives in this majestic mountain range.

Humboldt Bay National Wildlife Refuge:

Located on the northern coast of California, the Humboldt Bay National Wildlife Refuge encompasses diverse habitats, including salt marshes, mudflats, and coastal dunes. This refuge provides critical habitat for numerous bird species, including the endangered California clapper rail and the western snowy plover. Explore the refuge trails and observation platforms, where you can observe the incredible diversity of birdlife, including migratory shorebirds, waterfowl, and raptors. The refuge also supports a variety of mammals, such as river otters, beavers, and harbor seals. Visit the Humboldt Bay National Wildlife Refuge for a unique opportunity to witness the coastal biodiversity and engage in birdwatching and wildlife observation.

Mendocino Coast Botanical Gardens:

Situated on the scenic Mendocino Coast, the Mendocino Coast Botanical Gardens offer a unique blend of cultivated gardens and natural landscapes. Explore the various themed gardens, including the Rhododendron Garden, the Dahlia Garden, and the Perennial Garden, which showcase a stunning array of plant species. Take a stroll through the coastal bluffs and meadows, where you may encounter wildlife such as rabbits, deer, and a variety of bird species. The gardens' proximity to the coast also provides opportunities for marine wildlife sightings, including whales and seals. The Mendocino Coast Botanical Gardens offer a tranquil and captivating experience where you can connect with nature and appreciate the region's coastal flora and fauna.

Santa Cruz Wharf and Natural Bridges State Beach:

The Santa Cruz area is not only known for its vibrant beach culture but also for its diverse marine life. Take a walk along the Santa Cruz Wharf, where you can observe sea lions lounging on the docks and pelicans diving for fish. Visit Natural Bridges State Beach, a protected area known for its unique rock formations and tide pools. Explore the tide pools during low tide and discover an abundance of marine life, including starfish, sea anemones, and hermit crabs. Keep an eye out for dolphins and whales offshore, as these coastal waters are often visited by these magnificent creatures. The Santa Cruz Wharf and Natural Bridges State Beach provide a fascinating glimpse into the rich marine biodiversity of the region.

Cache Creek Natural Area:

Located in the Capay Valley, the Cache Creek Natural Area offers a picturesque landscape of rolling hills, canyons, and oak woodlands. The area provides habitat for a variety of wildlife, including deer, bobcats, coyotes, and a diverse range of bird species. Explore the numerous trails that wind through the natural area, offering opportunities for hiking, birdwatching, and wildlife observation. Cache Creek itself is a popular spot for kayaking, rafting, and fishing, with the possibility of spotting river otters and beavers along its banks. The Cache Creek Natural Area offers a peaceful retreat where you can reconnect with nature and appreciate the beauty of Northern California's landscapes and wildlife.

Northern California's wildlife and nature reserves provide a sanctuary for diverse ecosystems and a home for a remarkable array of wildlife species. Whether you're exploring ancient redwood forests, observing migratory birds in wetlands, or marveling at unique geological formations along the coast, these reserves offer a chanceto connect with nature, witness the wonders of wildlife, and appreciate the region's natural heritage. From the towering redwoods of the Redwood National and State Parks to the pristine shores of Point Reyes National Seashore, from the wetlands of the Sacramento National Wildlife Refuge Complex to the unique ecosystem of Mono Lake, each reserve offers a unique and captivating experience. So, grab your binoculars, pack your camera, and venture into Northern California's wildlife and nature reserves for an unforgettable journey through the region's natural wonders.

Romantic Getaways in Northern California

Northern California is not only a haven for outdoor enthusiasts and nature lovers but also a perfect destination for romantic getaways. From the picturesque coastline and charming coastal towns to the serene vineyards and luxurious retreats, the region offers a wealth of options for couples seeking a romantic escape. In this chapter, we will guide you through some of the most enchanting and idyllic destinations in Northern California, ensuring that you create unforgettable memories with your loved one.

Napa Valley:

Renowned for its world-class wineries and breathtaking landscapes, Napa Valley is a quintessential romantic destination. Take a leisurely stroll through the vineyards, hand in hand with your partner, and indulge in wine tastings at renowned wineries. Enjoy a romantic picnic amidst the rolling hills, or embark on a hot air balloon ride for a bird's-eye view of the stunning valley. Treat yourselves to a romantic dinner at one of the many acclaimed restaurants that offer farm-to-table cuisine paired with exceptional wines. Napa Valley sets the stage for a romantic and unforgettable getaway.

Mendocino:

Nestled along the rugged coastline, the charming town of Mendocino exudes a tranquil and romantic atmosphere. Explore the picturesque streets lined with Victorian-era cottages, art galleries, and boutique shops. Walk hand in hand along the cliffside paths that overlook the dramatic Pacific Ocean, and marvel at the breathtaking sunsets. Take a romantic horseback ride along the beach, or embark on a scenic hike in the nearby state parks. Stay in a cozy bed and breakfast or book a romantic inn with ocean views. Mendocino offers a peaceful and romantic retreat for couples seeking tranquility and natural beauty.

Lake Tahoe:

Surrounded by the majestic Sierra Nevada Mountains, Lake Tahoe is a stunning destination for couples year-round. In the summer, enjoy leisurely boat rides on the crystal-clear waters, relax on secluded beaches, or hike the scenic trails that offer panoramic views of the lake. In the winter, hit the slopes at world-class ski resorts, cuddle up by a cozy fireplace in a cabin, or soak in hot springs surrounded by snow-capped mountains. Lake Tahoe's natural beauty and abundance of outdoor activities provide the perfect backdrop for a romantic getaway in any season.

Carmel-by-the-Sea:

Known for its charming streets, pristine beaches, and artistic atmosphere, Carmel-by-the-Sea is a romantic paradise on the Central Coast. Take a romantic stroll along the white-sand beaches, explore the town's art galleries and boutiques, and enjoy a gourmet picnic in one of the scenic parks. Visit the famous Mission Ranch, owned by actor Clint Eastwood, for a romantic dinner overlooking the rolling hills. Carmel-by-the-Sea's European-inspired village and idyllic coastal setting make it a perfect destination for couples looking for a romantic and relaxed getaway.

Sonoma:

Located just next to Napa Valley, Sonoma offers a more laid-back and intimate setting for a romantic retreat. Explore the charming town square, filled with boutiques, tasting rooms, and cozy cafes. Visit the historic Sonoma Plaza, where you can enjoy a picnic or rent bicycles to explore the scenic countryside. Take a romantic drive through the vineyard-dotted landscape, stopping at wineries to sample award-winning wines. Stay at a luxurious wine country inn or book a private cottage nestled among the vineyards. Sonoma's rustic charm and world-class wines create an unforgettable romantic experience.

Half Moon Bay:

Escape to the coastal beauty of Half Moon Bay, where miles of pristine beaches and scenic cliffs provide a serene backdrop for a romantic getaway. Take a leisurely walk along the coast, collect seashells on the beach, or enjoy a romantic picnic with panoramic ocean views.Embark on a scenic drive along the Pacific Coast Highway, stopping at scenic overlooks and charming coastal towns. Indulge in fresh seafood at waterfront restaurants, or book a couples' spa treatment at one of the luxurious resorts. Half Moon Bay's coastal charm and tranquility make it an ideal destination for couples seeking a romantic coastal retreat.

Sausalito:

Located just across the Golden Gate Bridge from San Francisco, Sausalito offers a romantic escape with its picturesque waterfront setting and charming Mediterranean-style architecture. Take a romantic walk along the marina, admiring the sailboats and enjoying views of the San Francisco skyline. Explore the town's art galleries, boutique shops, and waterfront restaurants. Enjoy a scenic ferry ride to San Francisco, where you can visit iconic landmarks such as the Golden Gate Bridge and Alcatraz Island. Sausalito's romantic ambiance and proximity to the city make it a perfect base for exploring both natural and urban attractions.

Big Sur:

For couples seeking a truly breathtaking and secluded retreat, Big Sur is a dream destination. The rugged coastline, dramatic cliffs, and towering redwoods create a magical and romantic atmosphere. Explore the scenic coastal drives, such as the famous Pacific Coast Highway, which winds its way along the cliffs offering awe-inspiring views. Relax in hot springs overlooking the ocean, hike through ancient forests, or enjoy a private beach picnic. Unwind at a luxury resort perched on the cliffs, where you can soak in stunning sunsets and enjoy the serenity of nature. Big Sur's natural beauty and seclusion make it an unforgettable destination for couples seeking a romantic escape.

Healdsburg:

Nestled in the heart of Sonoma County's wine country, Healdsburg is a charming town known for its world-class wines, gourmet restaurants, and picturesque vineyards. Take a romantic bike ride through the rolling hills, stopping at wineries for tastings and picnics among the vineyards. Explore the town's quaint boutiques, art galleries, and tasting rooms. Indulge in farm-to-table cuisine at acclaimed restaurants, where local ingredients are showcased in exquisite dishes. Stay at a boutique hotel or a cozy bed and breakfast, and enjoy the peaceful ambiance of wine country. Healdsburg offers a perfect blend of romance, wine, and natural beauty.

Russian River:

The Russian River region, located in Sonoma County, is a romantic destination known for its scenic beauty and outdoor activities. Float down the Russian River on a canoe or kayak, enjoying the tranquility of the water and the lush surroundings. Explore the charming towns of Guerneville and Jenner, where you can visit local wineries, browse art galleries, or relax on riverfront beaches. Take a romantic hike through the redwood forests or along coastal trails. The Russian River's serene ambiance and natural beauty make it an ideal destination for couples seeking a romantic escape.

Northern California offers an array of romantic getaways, each with its own unique charm and allure. Whether you prefer the tranquil vineyards of Napa Valley, the coastal beauty of Mendocino, the mountain retreats of Lake Tahoe, or the charming towns along the coastline, Northern California provides the perfect backdrop for a romantic and unforgettable experience with your loved one. So, pack your bags, embrace the romance, and create lasting memories in the enchanting landscapes of Northern California.

Hot Springs and Wellness Retreats in Northern California

Northern California is a haven for those seeking relaxation, rejuvenation, and a connection to nature. With its geothermal activity and abundant natural beauty, the region is home to a variety of hot springs and wellness retreats that offer a perfect escape from the stresses of everyday life. In this chapter, we will explore some of the most enchanting hot springs and wellness retreats in Northern California, where you can immerse yourself in healing waters, indulge in spa treatments, and embrace a holistic approach to wellness.

Harbin Hot Springs:

Nestled in the Mayacamas Mountains of Lake County, Harbin Hot Springs is a renowned wellness retreat that has been attracting visitors for over a century. The natural hot springs on the property provide a therapeutic experience, with pools of varying temperatures that promote relaxation and rejuvenation. In addition to the hot springs, Harbin offers a range of wellness activities, including yoga and meditation classes, massage and bodywork sessions, and workshops on holistic healing. The serene natural surroundings and tranquil atmosphere make Harbin Hot Springs a true sanctuary for those seeking a wellness retreat.

Esalen Institute:

Located in Big Sur, overlooking the stunning

coastline, the Esalen Institute is a world-renowned retreat center that focuses on personal growth, healing, and self-exploration. Esalen offers a unique hot springs experience, with cliffside baths that allow guests to soak in the therapeutic waters while enjoying breathtaking ocean views. The institute also offers a variety of workshops and classes, ranging from yoga and meditation to dance and expressive arts. Immerse yourself in the healing power of nature, participate in transformative workshops, and enjoy the tranquil beauty of Big Sur at the Esalen Institute.

Wilbur Hot Springs:

Tucked away in the remote foothills of the Coast Range, Wilbur Hot Springs offers a peaceful and rustic setting for a rejuvenating getaway. The natural mineral hot springs at Wilbur are renowned for their healing properties and are open to guests 24/7. Unwind in the outdoor tubs, surrounded by the serene beauty of the landscape. Wilbur also offers accommodations in cozy cabins and a variety of wellness activities, including yoga and meditation classes, massage therapies, and nature hikes. Escape the noise of the modern world and embrace the simplicity and tranquility of Wilbur Hot Springs.

Orr Hot Springs Resort:

Nestled in the rolling hills of Mendocino County, Orr Hot Springs Resort is a hidden gem that offers a serene and relaxing retreat. The natural hot springs at Orr are renowned for their healing mineral waters, which can be enjoyed in a variety of private and communal tubs. The resort also offers massage therapy, yoga classes, and meditation spaces, allowing guests to further enhance their wellness experience. Immerse yourself in the peaceful surroundings, unwind in the hot springs, and rejuvenate your mind, body, and spirit at Orr Hot Springs Resort.

Indian Springs Calistoga:

Located in the charming town of Calistoga, Indian Springs is a historic hot springs resort that has been welcoming guests since the late 1800s. The resort features a large mineral pool fed by geothermal waters, as well as private mud baths and a spa offering a range of therapeutic treatments. Indian Springs also boasts beautifully landscaped grounds, including olive groves and gardens, creating a tranquil and picturesque setting. Enjoy a soak in the mineral pool, indulge in a mud bath, and immerse yourself in the charm and relaxation of Indian Springs Calistoga.

Vichy Springs Resort:

Vichy Springs Resort, located in Ukiah, is home to the only naturally carbonated Vichy mineral baths in North America. These unique baths offer a soothing and invigorating experience, as the effervescentwaters gently massage your body. The resort also features private hot tubs, a swimming pool, and a spa offering a range of wellness treatments. Vichy Springs Resort is surrounded by beautiful gardens and lush landscapes, providing a serene and rejuvenating atmosphere. Unwind in the mineral baths, explore the grounds, and embrace the healing powers of Vichy Springs.

Sierra Hot Springs:

Tucked away in the scenic Sierra Nevada Mountains, Sierra Hot Springs offers a peaceful and natural retreat for those seeking relaxation and healing. The resort features several natural hot spring pools, each with its own unique temperature and ambiance. Guests can also enjoy a variety of healing arts, including yoga classes, meditation sessions, and massage therapies. Surrounded by pristine forests and mountain vistas, Sierra Hot Springs provides a serene and tranquil environment for reconnecting with oneself and embracing wellness.

Tassajara Zen Mountain Center:

Located deep in the Ventana Wilderness, Tassajara Zen Mountain Center offers a truly unique and immersive wellness experience. As part of the San Francisco Zen Center, Tassajara focuses on Zen Buddhist teachings, meditation practices, and mindfulness. The center features natural hot springs that are open to guests, allowing for a serene and meditative soak in the healing waters. In addition to the hot springs, Tassajara offers meditation and mindfulness retreats, yoga classes, and gourmet vegetarian meals. Immerse yourself in the Zen teachings, enjoy the therapeutic hot springs, and embrace a holistic approach to wellness at Tassajara Zen Mountain Center.

Osmosis Day Spa Sanctuary:

Located in the picturesque town of Freestone, Osmosis Day Spa Sanctuary offers a unique and tranquil retreat for relaxation and rejuvenation. The spa is known for its signature Cedar Enzyme Bath, a therapeutic treatment where guests soak in a warm mixture of cedar and rice bran, promoting detoxification and relaxation. Osmosis also offers a variety of massages, facials, and body treatments inspired by traditional Eastern healing practices. Explore the beautiful gardens, relax in the peaceful surroundings, and indulge in the therapeutic treatments at Osmosis Day Spa Sanctuary.

Ratna Ling Retreat Center:

Nestled in the redwood forests of Sonoma County, Ratna Ling Retreat Center offers a serene and spiritual retreat for those seeking relaxation and personal growth. The center offers a variety of retreats and workshops focused on meditation, yoga, and mindfulness. Guests can enjoy the outdoor hot tub, sauna, and beautiful walking trails amidst the tranquil forest. Ratna Ling Retreat Center provides a peaceful and rejuvenating environment to reconnect with oneself and embrace a holistic approach to well-being.

Whether you're seeking a soak in healing hot springs, a tranquil and meditative retreat, or a rejuvenating spa experience, Northern California offers a range of options to cater to your wellness needs. So, let go of the stress and immerse yourself in the healing waters, serene landscapes, and holistic practices of the region's hot springs and wellness retreats. Embrace relaxation, rejuvenation, and a deep connection to nature in Northern California's wellness havens.

Northern California's Festivals and Events

Northern California is known for its vibrant and diverse cultural scene, and throughout the year, the region comes alive with a multitude of festivals and events that celebrate art, music, food, wine, and more. These gatherings not only showcase the unique heritage and creativity of the area but also provide a great opportunity for locals and visitors alike to immerse themselves in the lively atmosphere and vibrant community spirit. In this chapter, we will explore some of the most exciting and popular festivals and events in Northern California, ensuring that you don't miss out on the region's vibrant cultural offerings.

Outside Lands Music and Arts Festival:

Held annually in San Francisco's Golden Gate Park, the Outside Lands Music and Arts Festival is a three-day celebration of music, art, food, and wine. The festival features a diverse lineup of renowned musicians and bands across multiple stages, offering a range of genres to suit every taste. In addition to the music, attendees can enjoy art installations, interactive exhibits, and a wide variety of gourmet food and craft beverages from local vendors. With its scenic location and eclectic lineup, Outside Lands has become one of the most anticipated music festivals in the region.

BottleRock Napa Valley:

BottleRock Napa Valley combines music, wine, food, and art to create an unforgettable experience in the heart of California's wine country. This three-day festival showcases a mix of top-tier musical acts, including rock, pop, hip-hop, and alternative genres. Attendees can also sample wines from local vineyards, indulge in gourmet cuisine prepared by renowned chefs, and explore art installations and exhibits. BottleRock Napa Valley offers a unique blend of entertainment and culinary delights, making it a must-visit event for music and wine enthusiasts.

Monterey Jazz Festival:

Recognized as one of the longest-running and most prestigious jazz festivals in the world, the Monterey Jazz Festival attracts jazz lovers from far and wide. Held at the Monterey County Fairgrounds, the festival showcases renowned jazz musicians and emerging talent across multiple stages. Attendees can enjoy performances that span various subgenres of jazz, from traditional to contemporary, and participate in educational workshops and seminars. The Monterey Jazz Festival provides a unique opportunity to immerse yourself in the rich and soulful sounds of jazz in a picturesque coastal setting.

Sonoma County Hot Air Balloon Classic:

Take to the skies and experience the beauty of Sonoma County from a different perspective at the Sonoma County Hot Air Balloon Classic. This annual event brings together hot air balloon enthusiasts for a weekend filled with colorful and awe-inspiring balloon flights. Attendees can witness the launch and inflation of balloons, take tethered rides, and enjoy family-friendly activities such as live music, arts and crafts, and delicious food. The Sonoma County Hot Air Balloon Classic offers a whimsical and enchanting experience for all ages.

Gilroy Garlic Festival:

Celebrating the pungent bulb that is a staple of the region's agriculture, the Gilroy Garlic Festival is a culinary extravaganza that attracts garlic lovers from near and far. Held in Gilroy, known as the "Garlic Capital of the World," this three-day event showcases a wide array of garlic-infused dishes prepared by local chefs, as well as cooking demonstrations, live entertainment, and a variety of arts and crafts vendors. From garlic ice cream to garlic bread, the Gilroy Garlic Festival offers a unique and flavorful experience for food enthusiasts.

San Francisco International Film Festival:

As one of the oldest film festivals in the Americas, the San Francisco International Film Festival is a premier event for cinephiles and industry professionals. Over the course of two weeks, the festival showcases a diverse selection of films from around the world, including independent, documentary, and international cinema. Attendees can enjoy screenings, Q&A sessions with filmmakers, panel discussions, and special events. The festival provides a platform for emerging filmmakers and promotes dialogue and appreciation for the art of filmmaking.

California State Fair:

The California State Fair, held annually in Sacramento, is a celebration of the state's culture, agriculture, and entertainment. This multi-week event features a wide range of attractions, including live music performances, carnival rides, agricultural exhibits, and culinary competitions. Visitors can indulge in classic fair foods, explore interactive exhibits, and enjoy nightly fireworks displays. The California State Fair offers fun and entertainment for the whole family, highlighting the diverse offerings and achievements of the state.

Shakespeare in the Park:

Immerse yourself in the works of William Shakespeare at one of the many Shakespeare in the Park events held throughout Northern California. These outdoor theatrical performances bring the works of the renowned playwright to life in beautiful natural settings, allowing audiences to enjoy classic plays under the open sky. From San Francisco's Presidio to Sacramento's William Land Park, Shakespeare in the Park offers a unique and enchanting cultural experience.

Sacramento Music Festival:

Formerly known as the Sacramento Jazz Jubilee, the Sacramento Music Festival is a four-day celebration of music that encompasses a variety of genres, including jazz, blues, swing, rock, and more. Multiple stages throughout downtown Sacramento host performances by local and international musicians, offering a diverse and vibrant musical experience. In addition to the music, attendees can enjoy delicious food, browse arts and crafts vendors, and participate in dance lessons and workshops. The Sacramento Music Festival is a beloved event that brings the community together through the power of music.

Mendocino Coast Whale & Jazz Festival:

Combining two beloved aspects of the region, the Mendocino Coast Whale & Jazz Festival celebrates the migration of gray whales and the soulful sounds of jazz music. Held in Mendocino County, this month-long festival features concerts, art exhibits, lectures, and whale-watching excursions. Attendees can enjoy performances by local and visiting jazz musicians, explore the stunning coastal landscapes, and witness the majestic gray whales as they migrate along the Pacific coast. The Mendocino Coast Whale & Jazz Festival offers a unique blend of natural beauty and musical artistry.

These are just a few of the many festivals and events that take place throughout the year in Northern California. Whether you're a music enthusiast, a foodie, an art lover, or simply looking to embrace the cultural richness of the region, there is a festival or event to suit your interests. So, mark your calendar, embrace the lively atmosphere, and join in the celebration of Northern California's vibrant cultural scene.

A Farewell to Northern California: Reflections and Memories

As your journey through Northern California comes to an end, it's time to reflect on the experiences, memories, and the profound impact this remarkable region has had on you. From the awe-inspiring landscapes and vibrant cities to the rich cultural heritage and warm hospitality, Northern California leaves an indelible mark on the hearts of those who have explored its wonders. In this final chapter, we invite you to join us in bidding farewell to Northern California, while cherishing the memories and reflecting on the beauty and essence of this captivating destination.

Northern California is a place of contrasts, where rugged mountains meet the Pacific Ocean, and bustling cities coexist with serene wilderness. It is a region that offers a myriad of experiences, from hiking through ancient redwood forests to sipping world-class wines in picturesque vineyards. It is a place where you can immerse yourself in vibrant art scenes, indulge in delectable cuisine, and witness breathtaking natural wonders. The diversity of Northern California is what makes it so special, leaving a lasting impression on those who have had the privilege to explore its hidden gems.

Reflecting on your time in Northern California, you may find yourself reminiscing about the iconic sights that have taken your breath away. The towering redwoods of Muir Woods and the majestic granite cliffs of Yosemite National Park stand as testaments to the grandeur of nature. The iconic Golden Gate Bridge in San Francisco and the stunning coastline of Big Sur evoke a sense of wonder and inspire contemplation. The memories of gazing at the star-filled sky in the Sierra Nevada Mountains or witnessing a vibrant sunset over Lake Tahoe will forever be etched in your mind.

But Northern California is more than just its breathtaking landscapes; it is also a region rich in culture, art, and innovation. From the world-class museums and galleries of San Francisco to the cutting-edge technology companies of Silicon Valley, Northern California is a hub of creativity and progress. The music festivals, film screenings, and artistic performances that fill the calendar create an atmosphere of vibrancy and celebration. The culinary scene, influenced by diverse cultures and abundant local produce, tantalizes the taste buds and offers a gastronomic journey like no other.

However, it is the people of Northern California who truly make this region special. The warm and welcoming nature of the locals, their love for their land, and their passion for sharing their stories and traditions create an atmosphere of connection and community. The encounters with kind-hearted individuals along your journey, the conversations shared, and the friendships formed serve as a reminder that the true beauty of a place lies in its people.

As you bid farewell to Northern California, take a moment to appreciate the lessons and insights gained from your travels. The serenity of nature has taught you the importance of conservation and the need to protect the environment for future generations. The vibrant arts and cultural scene have ignited your own creativity and appreciation for diverse forms of expression. The culinary experiences have expanded your palate and inspired you to explore the flavors of other destinations. The encounters with different communities and their stories have deepened your understanding of the human experience.

While your physical journey may be coming to an end, the memories and experiences you have gained will stay with you forever. The photographs you captured, the flavors you savored, the moments of awe and wonder, and the connections you made with both nature and people will serve as a reminder of the transformative power of travel.

As you close this chapter on your Northern California adventure, take a moment to express gratitude for the opportunity to have explored this remarkable region. Cherish the memories, keep the spirit of Northern California alive within you, and allow the lessons learned and the experiences gained to shape your future journeys. Farewell, Northern California, until we meet again, and may the memories of your beauty andspirit continue to inspire and enrich our lives.

Printed by BoD™in Norderstedt, Germany